CW00869523

FUCKED BY ROCK

CREDITS

FUCKED BY ROCK
by
Mark Manning
ISBN 1-84068-026-1
Published 2001 by Creation Books
www.creationbooks.com

Cover photo/author photo (page 11):
Michael Chumiskey
Additional photos:
Marc Atkins, Steve Double, Annie Adjchavanich, Ken Copsey
All photos supplied from the Zodiac archive

CONTENTS

PREFACE:
MY WORST FRIEND
by
Bill Drummond

This morning I got a letter from Creation Books. They informed me they were going to publish a book called *Fucked By Rock – The Mindwarp Years* by my fellow literary arsehole, Arctic Explorer and worst friend, Z. They wanted to know if I'd write a preface for the book, "approximately 2,000 words would be great".

Well I've agreed, but only because I can use it as a platform to flaunt some of my many prejudices on the subject of rock and roll.

I'll start by stating three fundamental truths that you must not lose sight of while reading this book (which, as I write, I've not read either).

One – Rock'n'roll is both the highest and lowest art form that the last century has bequeathed to the lot of man.

Two – No musician has ever been ripped off by the music business. Having been ripped off is an illusory comfort blanket that musicians cling to when their dreams of endless wealth and unfaltering critical respect have not been achieved. Moreover, musicians have a tendency to rip *each other* off without a qualm.

And Three – Zodiac Mindwarp is the greatest rock star in the history of

MARK MANNING

Western culture.

In the telling of this tale, I will make no apology for shifting the goal posts, playing loose with the facts and indulging in the benefit of hindsight.

In the summer of '85 my long-term friend and sometime collaborator, Dave Balfe, gave me a call. "Bill, I met this bloke on the bus today. He sort of knew I was in the music business. He gave me a cassette of a song he'd written and recorded on some primitive home recording gear. I've just listened to it. I think he's got something."

Balfe and I had a music publishing company called Zoo Music. Music publishers are in the business of finding, signing, and then developing the careers of songwriters. Songwriting and publishing are where the real money is in the music business. This wealth is created in various ways. One example is radio play. Every time a song gets played on radio the publisher of the song gets paid a wad of money that he then divides up with the songwriter. The performer/s of the song get(s) nothing. If you can write a song that gets played forever on the golden oldie stations you will never have to work again.

"So what are you saying Dave?"

"I think we should offer him a deal. Nothing big, maybe a couple of grand to help him get some gear and put a band together, see what happens."

"I'll come round your place this afternoon, you can play me the song. What's he called?"

"Mark something."

I should have known then, there has never been a Mark in the history of rock and roll that deserves a mention. Mark is a name devoid of any magic, sexual threat or hidden meaning. OK Marc Bolan, but that's just the exception that proves the rule. If Mark Chapman's parents had called him Bill he would never have felt any need to kill John Lennon.

"What's the song called?"

"Wild Child."

Even worse than Mark. There had already been four songs that I knew called "Wild Child", and all of them were shite. As a title "Wild Child" signified a severe lack of imagination in the mind of its creator.

That afternoon Balfe played me this "Wild Child" by this Mark Nobody. It too was shite. It was not only shite, it was boring. Rambling on and on, this Mark Anybody mumbling over some ham-fisted unoriginal two chord riff was

6

never going to make any future playlist of a golden oldie station.

"Forget it Dave. He ain't got it."

"I dunno Bill. When I met him on the bus he had a vibe about him. A real thing, vibe and intelligence."

"OK but look, no more than five hundred quid."

"And a guitar. He wants a guitar, one that looks like Jimi Hendrix's or something."

"OK."

And that was that. That was how my life got messed up with this Mark and has been for the past sixteen years and counting.

Mark Stephen Manning his name was on the contract, already signed, sealed and delivered to Zoo Music for the next three years for the paltry sum of five hundred quid and a guitar thrown in before I'd even met him.

Things got better. This Mark Manning, as it turned out, did have an imagination. He was going to call himself Zodiac Mindwarp and his band, whoever they might turn out to be, were to be called The Love Reaction.

Zodiac Mindwarp and The Love Reaction was the best band name I had ever heard in my life. It still is. If that Mark something or other had told Dave Balfe on the bus that he was Zodiac from Zodiac Mindwarp and The Love Reaction, I'd have told Balfe we should sign him for a hundred grand now without hearing the tape. I exaggerate, but not much.

When I finally did meet our protégé I refused to acknowledge that he was ever known as Mark or Stephen or Manning. He was Zodiac Mindwarp, always had been, and always would be. As far as I'm concerned only girls, poofs and his mother call him Mark.

From somewhere, three unlikely lads took on the mantle of being The Love Reaction. Whatever their past lives had been was now irrelevant, they were re-christened Cobalt Stargazer, Slam Thunderhide and Kid Chaos. Included in the baptism was a complete new wardrobe of psychedelic nazi biker chic, all lovingly masterminded by Zodiac. On looking at the contact sheet of the band's first photo session and a list of the titles of songs that Zodiac was in the process of penning, I knew this was as good as it gets. When there is so much in the promise, you know that delivery is an impossibility.

This was the high point of the career of Zodiac Mindwarp and The Love Reaction. This was before they had recorded a note. Before they had even played one shithole of a gig. When it was all still a glorious fantasy of how it

MARK MANNING

could be. It is within this glorious fantasy that I judge Zodiac Mindwarp to be the greatest rock star in Western culture. In the real world all rock stars are pathetic tossers. Even the kings of their trade prancing about the stadium stages of the American Mid West, in front of 100,000 baying fans, are just bit-part players. Bitter has-beens in the waiting, destined to spend the rest of their lives trying to rediscover whatever it was they had in the first place. Unable to accept that it wasn't their innate genius that sucked in the light. That in fact they were just a jigsaw piece that momentarily fitted the ever-shifting puzzle we call the zeitgeist.

I've just put a red pen through the rest of what I wrote. I've decided you've heard enough of my many prejudices on the subject of rock and roll. And if you haven't, I have. A streak of mean-minded bitterness seemed to be leaking from my pen and I didn't like what it said about me. So out it goes, heading for the wastebasket. Instead I will write this:

It is enough to note that Zodiac Mindwarp and his Love Reaction became one of the most glorious failures that the history of rock and roll gets littered with and that a form of friendship evolved between Z and myself. A form of friendship I would not wish on my ultimate enemy. A form of friendship that allows for the most heinous of crimes to be committed and the stupidest of follies to be constructed.

I will fast forward, past all the events that I assume this book details in Z's 100% bullet-proof prose. I will freeze-frame on the pair of us standing on top of the burnt out shell of the ———— Hotel, Kisangani. We had just spent three weeks grinding up the Congo River from Kisangani on an ancient steamboat. You may already know that Kisangani is the fabled inner station, the very heart of Conrad's novella "Heart Of Darkness". We stand there under a blank blue sky on the highest building in this sprawling African city. Below we can't see the city at all. The jungle has been busy reclaiming Kisangani. The sea of green has risen to cover all but a few of the city's buildings. There are little sounds of traffic.

We came here to confront Satan and demand our souls back, we came to tear down the walls of Eden, and we came to escape the suffocating demands of domesticity. We came here to research a book. Not this one, another one yet to come – *The Wild Highway*. We came because we were driven by our own dark hearts and of course, our stupidity.

I will take my finger off the freeze-frame button and let real time flow.

"I fuckin' blame you Bill."

"What do you mean? I thought you blamed Balfe for everything."

"No I blame Balfe for the music business stuff but I blame you for all this other stuff. For the very fact that we are standing up here, in this, the most dangerous and lawless city in the world, with no return tickets to civilisation, no armed guards, and no mini bar..."

"And?"

"And I blame you that we haven't met Lucifer or even Modutu. We have come all this way and fuck all has happened. We have no big story to tell. We haven't even seen any lions, elephants or gorillas, we would have done better going to Woburn Safari Park. This has been a complete waste of time and energy."

"But Z we came. We fuckin' came, that's what really matters."

"Nah Bill. Look, we both made a couple of half-decent records and some that are best forgot. We both had careers that most lads with rock'n'roll dreams would have killed for. For what? To be stuck in this shithole in the middle of Africa."

"So where should we be?"

"Either in some Malibu Mansion, destroying what's left of our minds on grade A cocaine, wondering why the pizza delivery boy has brought a pizza and not the whore we ordered over an hour ago..."

"Or?"

"Or sitting in The Ship on Wardour Street with our pints of Stella wondering how it all went wrong. Making plans to reform the band and trying to convince ourselves that the kids of today will go for our brand of stale rock'n'roll."

"Well Z, yet again, you are wrong. This is where we should be. There is no better place in the world to be than right here, right now."

"Why?"

"Fuck knows."

"You know what I hate about you?"

"Well?"

"It's your smug self-righteous arrogance. Just 'cause you sold a few more records than me, you think it gives you the right to say how things are regarding rock music. For a start your records weren't rock, didn't even have a guitar on them. Novelty dance records. Clever, I'll give you that but not rock'n'roll. I bet if we were both to write books about our life and times in the rock'n'roll trade, it would be my one that people would want to read, the one that would be remembered. The one that would have future modern classic writ large, large across every page."

I put my finger back on the fast forward and arrive at now (Spring 2001). We got out of Kisangani just before some evil bastard turned on the taps for the biggest blood bath known to modern man. Not only has Z long finished writing his half of *The Wild Highway*, while I'm still struggling with mine. He has also written this book. His story of a life in the rock trade. I've not read it yet, but I know there is no point in me trying to pick up the gauntlet he threw down on that rooftop. There is no way I could ever compete with the story that Z is about to tell us.

There is no point in me telling you what a genius I think he is, you will read it and either know I speak the truth or I'm full of shit. But believe every word Z tells you, because if you don't, the record will stop turning and, like Tinkerbell, the music will go out.

–Bill Drummond 2001

INTRODUCTION:
THAT DANGEROUS ROAD
by
Mark Manning

"The road of excess leads to the palace of wisdom," said some literary arsehole as he buggered, drugged, wanked and drank himself into a pant-shitting, vomiting stupor, ending up in some 19th century version of The Priory.

Well I'm afraid there was no tower of enlightenment at the end of my season in Hell. Season? I beg your pardon dear boy, *Une Saison d' Enfer*? Une Fucking decade mon Ami. Sleazing away on that rumbling highway into the pit of no return. Unless this famed palace of wisdom looks like The Arse and Racket rock club in Wardour Street, that is.

Nope, there was no palace of wisdom for us toilet soldiers of rock, no excuses and no regrets.

And I loved every hotel bed-shitting, punk rock bitch-shagging minute of it, loved every banging up, snorting, smoking, blacking out hour of it. I loved drinking to way beyond pukedom. Couldn't get enough of the acres of unlubricated buggery, watching those little punk rock bitches hobbling to the bus stop in the morning, tears in their eyes, biting their black lipstick, arses killing them. Oh yes my brothers and sisters, oh yes indeed. Puking on their tits, choking them on the bloodhammer.

MARK MANNING

Me and my fellow meta-degenerates weren't interested in justifying our truly dreadful behaviour to any fucking women's issues lezzers. If the cunts didn't like it, they could always call the cops when we let them go.

We revelled in it, competed at it, shone at it! Were absolutely fucking fabulous at it! Fucking darling!

Probably the only time we weren't breaking one law or another was when we were asleep. And even then, falling asleep drunk, drug-hard dick still speared in some under-aged Yank skank's shitty buggery socket, Cobalt had actually managed to commit statutory rape while asleep on the job – or was it me? Who cares?

If facts, dates, reasons, studio names and all that other factual trainspotting bogroll crap is your bag – then this book isn't.

All of this gory sexual horror story happened in a massive depraved walking dream. A nightmare that I shared and enjoyed with a cavalcade of the most thoroughly lawless desperadoes and complete and utter bastard arseholes that ever took that awesome first step into the kingdom of disrule and mayhem that is the rock and roll road...

We stumbled through an entire decade not knowing what time, day, country, continent, or even year it was. I couldn't even remember if I was married or not. Cobalt kept saying I was, but I thought he was trying to wind me up.

Not that it would have made even the slightest bit of difference if I had believed him, to that bloody, venereal cascade of rape, buggery, Satanism and horrific turd sex that turned our fourteen-wheeled Leviathan into a permanent, rolling 120 days of Sodom.

Shit, some of us even forgot our own names. That's how good it was.

Sleaze lovers, we were the Emperors of bad, nad-spurting, woman-abusing misogynistic bitch-killing, turd sex.

Not since Caligula and his funky spam-sucking, bum-shagging sister partied hearty in that disco inferno that was the fall of Rome had history been graced with such elegant degenerates as the Love Reaction.

In fact if there were two books that were the template for our bad fun then the first surely must have been that stunning catalogue of the final years of the Roman Empire when the games degenerated into the ultimate in dreadful parties, Daniel P Mannix's *Those About To Die, Salute You*. That sublime and gratuitous tome written about events long after those hunky gay Australian gladiators had been deemed too tame. When Roman bloodlust

could only be sated by spectacles that involved very young, very blonde, very German children. Their little, bald, Teutonic cunts and bumholes smeared with on-heat, monkey sex-gland snakeoil, running like fuck around The Circus Maximus trying to escape the ravenous bestiality of huge troops of sexually insane baboons! Far fucking out! Bring on the nubiles! Bring 'em on baby! Bring 'em on! Go Bubbles go! Fuck that dumb little Claudia Schiffer, Visigoth bitch to death! Yeehaw!

And second, of course, was that lovable old rogue, that naughty old scamp himself, that literary Mister Punch, old laughing boy himself – the good Marquis de Sade and his saucy comedy classic, *The 120 Days Of Sodom*... "That's the way to do it! That's the way to do it! Chop her cunt out! Ha! Ha! Ha! And eat it!"

I remember reading it when I was about thirteen and laughing so much I shat somebody else's pants.

Yep, gentle reader, for ten arse-shagging, virgin-despoiling years we were indeed the unrivalled Gods of sex, war and Kentucky Fried Chicken.

Gary Glitter? We shit him! The lowest of the low baby; lower.

How we laughed when Flash protested that we should at least wait until a kid had reached puberty before we gang-raped her to death. What a fucking girl!

Didn't he know South American kids reached puberty at a much younger age than their North American slut sisters?

A bit like Britain during the industrial revolution, when virgin-shagging was considered a completeley normal and healthy sport for most wealthy Victorian gentlemen. Anyway, enough of our cultural and historical precedents; we didn't need any excuses for our abuses.

Despite all the above bravado, however, if I am brutally honest, I must admit if I had known just exactly how dangerous all this rock and roll shit was I probably wouldn't have been quite as keen on selling my soul as cheaply as I did.

This shit could, and did, on many Stateside drunken gun-toting incidents get pretty fucking dangerous, for me anyway. I mean, fuck the rest of them. You could always get a new band and crew. But shit man, those gun things, they were fucking dangerous; messy as well.

For a white fender guitar – a fucking Squire as well – I pawned my immortal soul to the most hated and cheapest man in the entire cosmosodomistic music business, Dave the Whale Balfe. Ex-keyboard player for Liverpool psychedelic band of drippy ambisexuals, The Arsehole Gets Bummed And Explodes Brownly. I mean what kind of name is that for a band anyway?

It was only later that I learnt of the involvement of that king of Bum Thunder and sexual torture, the man with the most terrifying arse in England, Pongo Bill Drummond, in the shameful scam.

I liked the guitar because it looked like the one Jimi Hendrix played. I was disappointed though because when I played it, it didn't sound like him.

It did however sound like Marc Bolan, which more than compensated.

I mean as a career, on the surface the old Rocking doesn't appear to be that dangerous. A few deaths; Jimi of course, drowning on puke – nice one Jimi, really cool.

Jim Morrison, alcohol and poetry wanking, even better.

Keith Moon, complete alcohol-fuelled arseholeism, brilliant.

Janis Joplin, Southern Comfort and ultra-slaggism, not bad, for a chick.

Kurt Cobain, monstrous wife and bad aim... hmmm, not a classic.

All of these inspirational people however were, if we were to be honest, simply a bit too clumsy in the too-much-fun department. Kind of dumb accidents more than anything else, really.

But these cats had the dollars, they shifted big units, they could afford to have too much fun. I mean they made even more of the green stuff after they died. A precedent set by that king of toilet death, old smartie-pill rattling burgerboy, Elvis Presley himself.

A lesson not lost on the sperm-drinking child molestors of that dreadful hydra-headed monster, Cosmosodomistic Records. Old Cosmosodomistic realised that a few re-releases and some lowest common denominator hyperbole could canonise these pretty average, pretty fucking crap really, if we're honest, human beings into icons of rebellion for whole successive generations of thick teenagers.

Turn goofy semi-autistic retards into Pagan Gods for the impressionable, the young and the dumb.

A whole industry built on real hardcore US retardism and a corporate cynicism, unrivalled since the Italian branch of Cosmosodomistic Inc, The Mafia, organized the prohibition laws in twenties America. And more recently when the Cosmosodomistic branch of the CIA insidiously hooked nice innocent black people on crack and terrible sports clothes with

automatic weapons as fashion accesories.

Turning these nice ordinary church-going people into bitch-slapping, motherfucking niggaz overnight.

I mean, I should know about the pagan rock god shit. Thirteen years old, I bought the whole fucking bag. Drugs, drink, sex, get lost mother, I'm staying up really late tonight, I'm going to drink heroin, and I'm never going back to school again, ever!

"The young man walked dowwwnnn the hallway!...." I mimed along with Jim Morrison, listening on a pair of massive seventies headphones almost as big as my head. "Father I want to fuck you..." Boy, what a chump.

But those unit-shifting corporation poodles these days – debauchery? No my friend and fellow sleaze-lover, they're far too busy working on their omnisexual six packs down in the cosmosodomistic gym dungeons to be in the slightest way interesting. I mean, when was the last time Alice or Ozzy buggered a chicken or bit a walrus's head off?

But us rats slinking around at the real low-down, brown end of the game.

Us rats who never sold millions of units, us rats that refused to allow David Gobbler and all the rest of those Kosher, cosmosodomistic, anus-gargling überlords, those dollar faggots like Frankie Auschwitz, Nad Pickles, Boris Oberschtump and their Nagasaki, techno-ronin goon squads, fondle our young white bottoms. We upstanding heterosexual perverts who refused to wear leather chaps with the arses cut out and shit on their football field-sized glass coffee tables.

It is we who carry the canon of the black church of the Rock, we pagan descendants of our Roman ancestors, we who carry the true tales of the excesses, the deaths, and the wanking wounded.

The drug casualties and the plain insane, the desperate and the deluded, the divorced and the married alive, the bummed and the bummers.

We electric troubadors who witnessed on an unbelievably epic scale the buggery and bloody carnage, the ravaged, sexed-out, drugged-out, bummed-out bodies that lie dead, or as good as, sprawling along that long and bloody highway into Hell and beyond.

We brave men, brave men indeed who gave our lives willingly for our creed and our true fatherland, that wild-blasted wasteland, Rock and Roll. We who were truly, nobly, willingly and, strangely enough, with terminal beauty FUCKED BY ROCK.

MARK MANNING

NOW WE SALUTE OURSELVES, GLORYING IN THE SPUNK-STAINED SWASTIKA STENCH OF OUR FUCKING ELECTRIC BABYLON – AND FUCK EVERY GODDAMNED FUCKING ONE OF YOU WHO CAN'T TAKE A FUCKING JOKE!!!
SPREAD 'EM FOR THE NEW CHOCOLATE ORDER!
HEIL HITLER BABY! SIEG HEIL! REICH AND ROLL! SUCK MY FUCKING COCK!
BLOOD, SHIT, FIRE AND WANKING ÜBER ALLES!!

—Mark Manning 2001

IT ALL GOES HORRIBLY RIGHT

I didn't exactly say take this job and stuff it up your arse.

But I did quit, somewhat ceremoniously.

Sent all the transparencies and typography, black and white photographs and stuff back to the office, with a simple note saying I couldn't do this shit anymore, that I had a higher calling.

Something schizophrenic like that anyway.

The fact is I really enjoyed the job.

Really liked my bosses too, Tim Lott and Barry Cain, great guys, showed me every kindness and gave me more opportunities than I ever deserved.

The pay wasn't great but then again neither was I.

I had my own little office, where I could fuck around, jack off when I got bored, great.

The actual work was a piece of piss, just sticking bits of paper on cardboard, arranging pretty colours and drawing cartoons.

Its posh name was graphic designer.

I was working for a teenage pop magazine called *Flexipop*.

You know the kind of thing. Those colourful little rags that contribute to the complete and utter feelings of worthlessness that plague most teenagers' angst-driven existences.

I'm not accusing the editors of wilfully promoting the propaganda of envy.

The idea that someone, somewhere is having a better life than you.

That while you're on holiday with your parents in a leaky caravan just outside Bognor some other lucky girl is sailing in the Carribean with Duran Duran before they started looking like the corpses of Andy Warhol and Elvis Presley.

That while your father is farting over his turkey and vaporised sprouts, getting pissed and beating up your mother another lucky girl is skiing in the Alps.

Wrapped up warm in a fashionable ski suit enjoying a "last Christmas" with George Michael before he reveals that he much prefers wanking himself off in public bogs with strange ugly men than drinking mulled wine in Alpine ski lodges with Pepsi and Shirley.

I guess somehow this dreadful world of bogus glamour, all those videos of bands shagging thousands of women, Dave Lee Roth, Kiss, I somehow must

MARK MANNING

Young Zodiac contemplates a cosmosodomistic future

have bought it, somehow must have thought it was all true, that those ugly, retarded, hairy imbeciles really did get to shag all these glamorous women in far out places.

Boy was I wrong, as you can tell from this sordid collection of rocky horror stories.

MINDWARP

So there I was bumbling away in my office reasonably happy with enough money to get pissed every night and enough for a wrap or two of nuclear sulphate at the weekend.

But even though I was embroiled in the very cogs of the machine that promoted this propaganda of envy, this vile lie, this web of tacky illusion, this sinister conceit pushed by that evil cosmosodomistic corporation of the black gas, I bought it all hook line and sinker and I wanted some of that bogus candy, I wanted to *carpe* my *diem*, seize that foolish day.

I wanted to be a rock star.

I wanted to be the dirtiest, lousiest, most horrible evil bastard that ever trailed his diseases across the pizza-acne plateaus of planet rock.

I wanted to be a coruscating, shimmering hybrid constituted from the phantom charisma left hovering in the deceased wake of Adolf Hitler, Joan of Arc, Marc Bolan, Elvis Presley, Jim Morrison and Genghis Khan.

But how?

How do you get to be a rock star and shag thousands of women every weekend and bugger even more during the week?

It was going to need some heavy magic.

I decided to ask my friend Youth.

Youth was in an occult rock band called Killing Joke, they weren't exactly a shagging-type rock band, more into paranoia and Satanism, Aleister Crowley and other sinister Geomantic mushroom diversions.

If anyone could point me in the right directions it would be this drugged-out occult master of disaster.

Youth sorted out the pentagrams, called down some Earth spirits and we set the controls for the heart of the sun.

After the fifth hit of purple imbecile kicked in, shit started getting weird.

Really fucking weird.

I mean I'd read and heard about all that shrinking and gianting out shit like in Alice in Wonderland, but I'd never experienced it myself.

I'd seen the odd dancing skeleton and yes, dreadlocks can get quite serpentine, but this....

Youth looked at me, his eyes like fried eggs, his dreads a writhing nest of hissing serpents, tongues flickering, the fucking works.

Pointed teeth, a full gob of Dracula.

MARK MANNING

The huge spliff he'd rolled to try and take the edge off of all this psychedelic mayhem had telescoped into a massive curved scimitar.

"I think we're having a bad trip." His voice eight octaves below normal reverberating around the room like Hammer horror.

"A bummer," I added, sounding like Pinky and Perky in an echo chamber. "Oh fuck, oh fuck, put some music on!"

Now I don't know why, I mean AC/DC always used to make me feel good, happy, if you know what I mean, dancing around laughing and headbanging, but fuck, shit, *Highway To Hell*, it just sounded, I dont know, like kind of evil and Satanic.

But then again even Donovan's "Sunshine Superman" sounded creepy and weird, as if he was tripping on us some kind of weird subliminal Nietzsche/ Adolf Hitler shit.

"Maybe it's this place?" reverberated Youth, referring to the Dracula's castle ambience of the Coach House, his gothic Clapham abode. The decor was all writhing house plants and cats flying around, leaping out of the twisted Rousseau verdure.

This was around the time when the Goth scene was big, so there were like lots of skulls and other kack-handed Halloween-style martyred saint-type images dripping all over the walls.

We brave Psychonauts in a bid to save our sanity decided to take a hike across Clapham Common, maybe get like a rural countryside vibe going, what with the trees and grass and shit. Bad move. Really bad fucking move.

We opened the front door; there been a road accident immediately outside, flashing blue lights discoed away, lakes of shiny blood pooled in the gutters reflecting the yellow sodium street lighting.

The whole area was crawling with Fuzz.

Their evil drug offender detector hummed audibly amongst the carnage.

Youth slammed the door quickly, shut the curtains and turned out all the lights.

Suddenly the radio turned on all by itself.

Aliens had landed on the other side of the common.

We would have to tough it out till morning.

Unable to look at each other, our limbs had started disconnecting and millions of winged eyeballs were flying around the room; we took two blankets from the evil airing cupboard and hid beneath them for the next

fourteen hours, whimpering like mice.

LSD, eh kids? What a laugh.

We wound up on a beach in Formantera two weeks later, searching for something.

I didn't know what, I don't think Youth knew either.

But both of us found something.

Youth found some Hippy magic that enabled him to become one of the top producers in Britain, and Truman Capote answered my prayers.

Answered Prayers, is the title of the scabrous little tome that finally finished off the social-climbing literary snitch and opens with a quote from Saint Teresa: "More tears are shed over answered prayers than unanswered ones". The thing is however, neither Truman nor the grumpy old nun said exactly whose those tears would be. As for myself, all I know is that when my prayers were finally answered, the tears surely weren't mine.

I have an idea who did shed them though, I mean unlike suicide, buggery – eh ladies – that, I am told, can occasionally be quite painful.

Of course I'm being facetious, the road is not called the Highway to Hell for nothing.

And Saint Teresa is not the only one to have made that spooky observation. Ever since homo sapiens learned to scare the shit out of each other beneath full moons sat around camp fires there have been tales about deals with the devil going horribly wrong. How old Scratch grants a man his most urgent desire then sits laughing as the poor bastard's life goes straight down the shit-filled toilet.

Hello magazine documents the signings every week. The *Sun* newspaper and her tawdry sisters document the subsequent spiralling misery in the months and years that follow.

But of course on that weird Balearic island full of naked women and sangria, the last thing on my mind was the tragic consequences that are inevitably the result of too much fun.

I had a date with the Devil and I didn't want to be late.

Now it takes great skill to get stopped by coppers when you're *leaving* England.

On entry into the country with a suitcase possibly full of heroin and a child

MARK MANNING

prostitute concealed in your Y-fronts, yeah, I can see why they might not want that kind of thing in upstanding moral Britain.

But leaving upstanding moral Britain, why the fuck would they give a shit about what you were taking out of the place. After all who gives a shit in upstanding moral Britain if a bunch of Frogs or greasy Spaniards drop dead from heroin overdoses and the like.

But no, it was bumspoon time. Down with the pants and the cop with the worst job in the world was down on his knees with his shiny piece of cold metal and his little red maglite checking out what we'd had for breakfast.

Officer Arsesniffer didn't find anything though, Youth had swallowed the half ounce of paki black as soon as we were waved over into his creepy little office.

"Do you like your job?" I said to Officer Arsesniffer.

"Its OK," answered the anal detective defensively; the poor bastard couldn't have been more than twenty-three.

"I mean what kind of things do you find up people's arses, apart from farts and shit and stuff?" I said trying to sound genuinely interested.

"You'd be surprised sir," he said, slightly less warily.

"Drugs I suppose mainly," added Youth.

"Mainly drugs sir yes," he replied, taking off his rubber gloves and washing his hands. "But you do occasionally get people trying to smuggle other contraband items anally."

"Contraband?" Youth again, I think he liked the sound of the word, the paki black was obviously kicking in.

"Yes guns sir mainly, a lot of people try to smuggle guns up their arses," replied Sergeant Billy Bumsniff.

"What, loaded guns?" I asked incredulously, I mean I've heard of some pretty dumb things in my time, really dumb things, but a loaded gun up your jacksie? I dont even think Gimpo would have done something as stupid as that.

"Some of the Irish chaps sir yes, makes a terrible mess when they go off accidentally, terrible sir, some people sir, no consideration for others...." The man with the worst job in the world trailed off.

I suspected that he thought he was revealing too many bumhole trade secrets as he brusquely opened the door, looking a little flustered, and let us out.

FUCKED BY ROCK

"Your flight's in about ten minutes sir, you'll make it if you rush, have a nice trip," he called politely before going back into his little arse detective room.

After the first two disastrous days of being unable to find a hotel and sleeping in fields, Youth was completely, utterly, and totally fucked. He was raving about Freemasons and interstellar leylines, could hardly walk and had vomited over the one hotel check-in register that we nearly managed to secure. It must have been bad dope, he said pathetically when the ingested dosage wore off. We eventually found a humble little *pension* on the main drag of San Ferdanandos and set about going properly insane.

Well I did anyway.

Maybe it was all the acid I'd been crunching down on over the previous eleven years. Maybe it was some kind of breakdown brought on by the fact that I'd just jacked in a pretty reasonable job with an obvious career trajectory to chase some ludicrous dream without a clue as how to even reach first base. Maybe it was just the sun, who fucking knows. All I know is that my marbles seriously went missing out there on Witch Island.

But it was in the middle of all this breakdown crap – living in a tree for two days, communicating telepathically with the island's stray dogs, being haunted by electric cockerels, brain dribbling moonfear, howling like a fucking werewolf on midnight beaches, all the usual psychotic crap – that Zodiac Mindwarp finally appeared.

Youth had found the name in a catalogue list for underground sixties and seventies comic-books. It was by some biker cartoonist cat from San Francisco called Spain Rodriguez. I don't know why, there was something about it, all the right connections, the twelve signs of the zodiac, the twelve apostles, the twelve months of the year, it just seemed right.

Well that was the first stage – my muse had been given a name.

Of course, at the time I didn't realise that it was by way and far above more than a name. It was something elemental. Some strange pagan spirit that had decided to take a ride in my soul. Mostly benign, but capable of terrifying rages, a jealous spirit as well, if not tended everyday and allowed some form of creative expression.

There are strange forces at work on Formentera.

Just ask Syd Barrett. The ultimate fucked by rock icon.

Syd has a house on Formantera.

MARK MANNING

As do many other seriously fucked by rock icons.

So now that I had a name I decided that I had better make some kind of a demo tape.

I had no idea *how* to make a demo tape but that didn't bother me, I had no idea how to design a magazine when I applied for the job as graphic designer at *Flexipop*.

I winged it in the graphic design world and I was pretty sure I could wing it in the rock world.

I knew how to play two bar chords and I was pretty sure I could sing, it was just like shouting only with a tune wasn't it?

I had a friend in Bradford, a cat called Buzz who was in some weirdo goth band called Southern Death Cult. They were famous for having the most far-out haircuts the world had ever seen and also being extraordinarily handsome. Oh, they had a couple of tunes as well, something about a Moya and a Fat Man.

The last time I had talked to Buzz he had mentioned how he had bought a portastudio, which he kept in a small cellar beneath Roots record shop on Lumb Lane.

I packed some sandwiches and set off walking to Bradford.

Buzz was always pleased to see me – sort of. Like with most of my friends, I always detect a slight tinge of trepidation when I turn up unannounced on their doorsteps at midnight.

"You want me to drive you down into Bradford now and show you how to use a portastudio?" said my bleary-eyed friend on the doorstep of his Buttershaw Estate council flat.

"Yes, it's of utmost urgency, I am on a mission to save the world of rock," I answered in all earnesty. My feet were hurting, I'd just walked two hundred and fifty miles without a single beer.

"Mark, it's nearly three o'clock in the morning, I was just going to bed," he replied, wiping his eyes and yawning.

"Time is of no consequence to me, I am on urgent business, I have to save the world. Buzz, you must help me," I said, seriously.

"Oh for fuck's sake, hang on a minute, I'll get my car keys."

The Southern Death Cult guitarist tried to show me how to work the portastudio, failed, and losing his temper just left me to it. "Try not to break

anything will you," he said resignedly, and left me to it.

Eighteen hours I was in that damp, windowless cellar. I had a drum machine, a Tascam four-track portastudio, two manuals, one microphone, one amp, one Ibanez electric guitar, one fake Fender precision bass and a riff. I came out with a completeley unlistenable cacophonous eighteen-minute version of a track called "Wild Child".

I set off walking back to London without even thanking my friend. The world was my donut. As soon as Trevor Horn heard this, I thought, move over Frankie I'm coming to Hollywood.

After trekking over to Sarm West in Notting Hill and leaving my masterpiece for the king of all record producers to hear and immediately want to produce, I went back home and sat by my phone.

For a week.

The four-eyed talentless cunt never called.

The fact that my phone had been cut off a month earlier didn't even figure in the equation. Even less, the fact that I hadn't even left my phone number.

"Zodiac, hey man, what are you up to?" It was Dave Balfe, a man I was to share some of the best and worst times of my entire life with over the next five years.

I was sat on the top deck of the number thirty-eight bus on my way home to my Clerkenwell hovel. Balfe was sleazing off to some bird's house on the Bourne Estate, near to where I lived.

I'd met Dave a few months earlier through Youth, he was interested in me possibly doing some design work for his new Food label. I didn't have a folio and was completely unprofessional, so nothing came of it.

"Erm, I've done a demo, here look." I pulled out the only copy I had of "Wild Child" – I'd only made two, one for that fat four-eyed bastard Trevor Horn and one for myself.

I gave it to Dave and went back to sit next to my phone that didn't work.

"Wild Child" was an underground indie hit and I didn't even have a band.

Balfe cobbled together a ramshackle bunch of degenerates. Youth on bass, Jimmy KLF Cauty on guitar and Jake le Mesurier on drums. We played one gig at the King's Cross Water Rats and then I sacked them, they didn't take my divine calling seriously and like most people thought I was just a fucking lunatic. Assholes.

I had to get a real band. Balfe agreed.

But how?

As usual, these things, when they're supposed to happen, are usually just around the corner. You just have to look.

I'd fallen in love with a lesbian stripper, and in between bouts of completely disturbing drug-addled sex had mentioned my quandary.

Problem solved. Her best friend, another lesbian stripper, was having disturbing drug-addled sex with some cat called Cobalt Stargazer – apparently he was a guitarist.

The strippers arranged a meeting.

"So man, you like play guitar and shit?" I'm trying to remember verbatim what went down here, I think it's pretty accurate. Cobalt and myself never really pussyfoot around, just get straight to the point. That's why we don't have any friends.

"Erm yeah, I have a guitar and I can play it," said Cobalt warily, his eyes were kind of distant. I put it down to all the disturbing drug-addled sex he was having with his lesbian stripper.

"Right yeah," I said, trying to collect my thoughts. His lesbian stripper was writhing on the barstool saying something about how she hadn't had an orgasm in over two hours and how she would have to go to the toilet to masturbate.

My lesbian stripper went with her, leaving us to discuss business.

"So Cobalt, can you like make your guitar go, weeee, peownnnng, dooo doooo doooo grrrrrrounchh, like sort of Eddy Van Halen sort of shit?" I asked.

"Yeah, yeah, I can do all that, hammer-ons and stuff, fucking easy," answered the Stargazer nonchalantly.

"What about sort of grindy Marc Bolan sexy thrashy shit?" I enquired, already convinced of his credentials by the mere fact that he knew what I was talking about and the fact that his lesbian stripper was even filthier than mine.

"Look am I in the band or not?" he said impatiently. "It's just that, you know, I've got a lot of disturbing drug-addled sex to catch up on, we haven't done it for about two hours and I'm coming down fast."

The Stargazer looked twitchy. He was fucking in alright. And I hadn't even heard him play.

"Z, yeah it's me Dave, we got this letter this morning, some kid says he's a friend of Youth's." It was Balfe. He'd had my phone reconnected. It was really easy, he just payed the bill. That's the great thing about managers, they know how the real world works. I mean I would have sat there forever, taking the damn thing apart, messing with the wires, pouring jam into it, doing voodoo and shit to try and get it to work. But old Dave, what a fucking genius, just wrote a cheque and like wow, I'm connected.

"I don't really understand it, it's written in musician language, do you want to call into the office and check it out... I think he wants to play bass with you or something," said Dave. I could hear the sound of calculator machines and someone screaming about money in the background.

"My name is Kid Chaos, my bass guitar goes Zap! Twang! Thud! Surfing is my life," said the letter.

All we needed now was a drummer.

"You got a fucking problem buddy?" said the handsome Canadian in the rubber mini-skirt. Cobalt, Kid Chaos and myself were getting loose in some sleazoid, lesbian, heroin bar in Soho. It was about four in the morning and we were pretty much just getting our second wind. We'd switched from smack to crack and were feeling just dandy, the vodka martinis were stoking our engines real peach sideways.

Kid Chaos had turned out to be just fine. Not only did he have a lesbian stripper girlfriend, he had two. All four girls were getting jolly on the floor, fists up each others' arses, sucking on the furburgers, hairy pie all over the fucking place.

"Hey no man, we just wondered if you were like a drummer? You look like a drummer," said Kid Chaos placatingly.

"You saying I look fucking stupid or something you gay little bastard?!" shouted the colonial before throwing his drink in Kid's face, ripping down his rubber mini-skirt and taking a shit on the floor.

Mr. Slam Thunderhide; lead drums with the Love Reaction.

AND BUGGER THE CHARRED REMAINS

Believe it or not, I once believed I had a sense of morality.

I actually believed that out there in some vague Manichean cosmos there were forces of good and evil battling it out for the sake of the universe.

Like in a Marvel comic or the Koran or the Bible or some other rambling, poetic epic. What a fucking chump.

Well, I was kind of young. Which is as good an excuse for being a fucking idiot as any I suppose.

I thought that people should respect each other, be kind and gentle to each other.

One month in a rock and roll band soon knocked that shite clean out of my head.

I think it was probably more or less the crew that schooled all of us into the feral hinterlands of absolute degeneracy.

Gimpo, a battle-tested Argentinian war veteran, a man who truly enjoyed buggery and killing. Smithy, an ex-Marine, kicked out for his attitude, "refusing to soldier on" they called it. Kicking an officer in the balls was what Smithy called it.

Our fine Shutzstaffel silverback, Überstürmführer Smith, he too adored buggery and violence almost as much as the Gimp. Many's the crippled punk rock bitch I'd see limping from behind the amplifiers, holding her backside in agony as the monstrous bum-cleaver fastened up his leather trousers, lighting a fag, a big sodomistic smile on his face.

And Joe, a six-foot-six ex-BNP mixed race skinhead. None of those Nazi boy scouts dared mention Joe's distinctively non-Aryan parentage. As if I need say? Violence and punk rock bitch arse were also high on our brave storm-trooper's agenda, although with Joe it seemed that it was more the violence than the bumtorture he preferred.

Horses for courses I guess.

Joe's bloody preference probably had a lot to do with the insane amount of ice, crack and plain old amphetemine sulphate he used to crank up. The PCP and some other weird shit I've never even heard of. Well, if he wanted blood, he fucking got it.

I had no chance.

It was Kid Chaos and Cobalt that were the first to go.

Gimpo's jokes, which now amuse me no end. Swerving on country roads to get road kill, family cats, little ducks and stuff. Making the gesture to nail some schoolgirl on a bicycle with the quip "Knock her over, get her while she's still warm". Makes me laugh from the belly upwards just remembering it.

But at the time I was appalled.

We were the Love Reaction, we believed in peace, love and all that other deeply naïve, hippy horse shit.

It must have been some strange side effect left over from all the LSD I used to take back in the sixties.

When I was ten.

Listening to all that peace and love music like Alice Cooper, Iggy and the Stooges, Grand Funk Railroad and Ted Nugent.

Smithy's fierce intimidation of anyone whose face he didn't like, his baseball bat, his swastikas and shit all over the fucking place. He even wore the SS TOTENKOPFVERBANDE insignia of the death camp SS. Probably the most evil organisation ever to have ever existed on Satan's black Earth.

I may have been the singer, but it was Smithy's band.

Smithy's ferocity and mania for extreme bondage torture and deranged buggery sessions with punk rock bitches, which often stretched screaming long into the morning, was matched by Joe's pathological paranoia.

The mad brown bastard kept a loaded AK47 under his bunk and never seemed completely at ease other than when sharpening his collection of very large, already very sharp hunting knives lovingly on a whetstone.

It was the only thing that seemed to steady his teetering amphetamine psychosis.

Well Kid and Cobalt, they worshipped these guys, and had soon developed a sense of humour shared only by those Gallic laughing boys, the Marquis de Sade and Gilles de Rais.

I was struggling hard to keep some kind of balance. Surely this couldn't be right, all these rape jokes and blow by blow accounts of the squalid, cheesey bell-end sex and endless punk rock bitch bumming we'd already descended into.

The Croydon fuzzboxes. My God those poor little punkettes couldn't have been more than fourteen at least. We'd named them after a band of fun-

loving girls popular at the time. We've Got A Fuzzbox And We're Going To Use It they were called. "You've got a bumhole and I'm gonna shag it", Smithy used to call them.

Smithy had developed an unhealthy obsession with the young punkish females and I was seriously worried about what might happen to their ringpieces if we ever came across them on our travels.

He'd started collecting pictures of them and pinning them to the walls of his bunk.

He'd cut all of their bumholes out. It was scary, I tried not to think about it.

"No man," said Kid Chaos. "When you've fucked her arse really hard without even any spit or anything and definitely no Bum OK snakeoil and she's gone to put ointment up her bumhole to try and fix it, you nick all the money out of her handbag and then shit in it. That's what Smithy says anyway." I couldn't believe I was hearing this, the young lad was only seventeen – what perverse road to hell had I dragged him into?

"I thought you were supposed to shit on their faces after dosing them with Rohypnol," said Slam.

"No, no in their bags, then you give them the Rohypnol."

I couldn't stand it anymore. In that small cramped cabin on some ferry to somewhere, I finally flipped. "What the fuck is wrong with you fucking bastards!?"

The other three guys looked at me as if I was insane or something. I leapt from my bunk. "What's happening to us? We're supposed to be the Love Reaction – *love!* Yeah? Like being nice to people and shit," I shouted. Cobalt snickered.

"What next?" I said, trying to appeal to something human in these spiralling degenerates.

"We set the poor fucking bitches on fire and bugger the charred remains!"

"Sounds good!" laughed Kid Chaos, Cobalt and Slam.

I ran up on deck out into the icy Nordic night, confused, mind racing, trying to figure out where all this appalling attitude was taking us.

And then, I don't know why, maybe some Loki, Norse God of badness was fucking with me. I started laughing. Big fat belly laughs echoing up into that star mad sky. Shitting in her handbag, that *was* fucking funny. No spit and definitely no Bum OK snake oil?

Punk rock bitches. Why punk rock bitches? Why did you only bugger punk

rock bitches? I don't know why, it just seemed so fucking funny. I was laughing like a lunatic, eager to bugger a punk rock bitch at the very first opportunity.

I had surrendered to something evil, joyous, wicked and wild, deep inside of me.

We were on that highway that's for sure, the one that Bon Scott and AC/DC sung about. The one to Hell.

And I confess now, with no shame. It felt good. Fucking good.

I ripped off the ring pull of some shitty ferry beer and decked it in one. Toasted the moon and threw the can into that black sea, laughing like a madman.

"You won't feel my dick till it's hanging out your arse" I sang, changing the lyrics to that AC/DC classic, "Night Prowler". "You PUNK ROCK BITCH!" Imitating the demonic scream of that wild Australian descendant of Cain. That dead Satanic legend, Bon Scott. I almost fell over the railing I was laughing so much.

Someone said that rock and roll was the Devil's music.

I tell you friend, they were fucking right.

And I'll see you in Hell.

You punk rock bitch.

LOVE ON THE ROAD

Was simply not allowed.

Any sign of affection shown to a member of the opposite sex was greeted with complete and absolute adolescent derision.

I don't know whether it is something particular about the rocking, or whether this type of attitude and behaviour infects all groups of men denied the company of women for long periods. I mean my old man worked on oil rigs, and some of the shit he told me about those isolated worlds of testosterone and builder's arse cracks...

I mean rocking, I'm sorry girls, but it's a man's job. I still find the sight of a woman with a guitar and a sneer not only unsightly, but deeply sad and even more deeply unsexy.

A chick with a guitar – man, I'd rather fuck Smithy.

Which brings me neatly around to what amused me this morning as I lay in bed with my permanent partner, hangover, the bitch.

We were somewhere, possibly America.

The Smith had it bad. Fucking roses, everything. He's like got this shave, *doesn't* stink of drugs, beer breath, piss, grease, farts and electricity. I think the motherfucker must have even had a bath, which is saying something as the big fat fucker is almost as bad a soap dodger as me.

He's even ditched his death camp drag, not a swastika in sight. Hair neatly combed.

In a little ponytail and everything.

Dining out with his ladyfriend. Tastes the wine without laughing, nods politely and pours the bint a glass. Candles and shit, soft music. The perfect romantic dinner.

Except on the next table was us rotten fuckers.

Me, The Count, The Gimp, Slam and Kid Chaos. Trying real hard not to laugh.

Smithy's eyes keep flicking over towards us, suspiciously, as we nearly bust our guts stifling our mean laughter. You fucking girl Smith. Smithy knows that this is what we all are thinking, and that as soon as lady love is out of the place we're going to rip the shit out of him mercilessly for fucking days.

"Alright Rosey?" Kid Chaos started it the next day, refering to the dopey bastard's little flower gift. Fuck man, chicks are modern these days, they

drink pints, they don't buy all that romantic crap.

"Fuck off!" He glowered and busied himself behind an amp. Well, that was it. It was open season on loverboy. The Count, Cobalt, mimicking pouring glasses of wine and drinking them with a crooked little finger.

"Do you love her Smithy?" grinned Slam, daring the humongo, beast, arsemaster road warrior to show the slightest trace of humanity. I mean this was the king of punk rock bitch bumming, the übersodomist who fucked chicks so hard they pissed the bed. Buggered them so savagely they shit all over the fucking place once he'd hammered them with the oyster.

And here the big fucking woman was, completely letting the side down. Flowers? Wine? I mean I bet he fucked her really politely as well, didn't force her to suck his stinky bell-end, or shove her one up the khyber, or call her a cunt and throw her out of the window after the dreadful deed was done. I mean I reckon the big jessie even had her fucking phone number, knew her second name, and was going to call her when he got off tour. Well, not if we could fucking help it.

We found the picture of her taped in his bunk, the arse not ripped out or anything. He obviously lay there mooning over the stupid yank cunt, thinking romantic arse about her. What a fucking chump, love on the road.

Obviously I can only be this mean about a fellow arsemeister road warrior because I too – may deep shame pour on me from the rock heavens – have commited the terrible sin of love on the road. Have seen the stifled laughter and utter contempt from my arsemeister colleagues as I frolicked in the Norwegian snow with some cunt who caught me sentimental. Missing that rare thing, a woman's touch.

Two months on that rolling barnyard with the most horrible men on the planet, all stinking of leather trousers, bad breath, arsegrease, farts, wanking and swearing. Swastikas and knives, guns and beer, whiskey, dirty hair and drugs, all over the fucking place. Violent video games, *Mortal Kombat* for seriously demented lengths of time. From London to Switzerland we tried to get that Goro cunt down. Didn't even notice the ferry, the Alps, beer, beer, beer, spliff, spliff, spliff, FIGHT! Excellent! says the master. Good Lord, I mean, OK, if we were fourteen it would be completely normal, but we were grown men, in our thirties. What is it about the Rock that retards you immediately that eight-wheeled old rolling sodom tourbus turns up?

Actually, I've been prey to love on the road on more than one occasion.

Do not philosophise with a sledgehammer.. Use an electric guitar

MARK MANNING

But don't tell anyone.

It's a rare and strange thing this fast love business.

And, dare I even confess, it can also be quite wonderful.

I mean I have to confess – if the truth be known – I can't fuck a woman unless I feel something within a mile or two of love. I'm just weak that way. I have to like them at least. The old Stargazer, he doesn't have that problem at all; fat birds, old, ugly bitches, that motherfucker he can fuck them all. Tex as well, anything. I must admit I find it impressive, the ability to throw an oyster up anything you can hold down long enough. It's not as easy as you think, especially for a big High Priest of Love, King of Sex like me.

Nope, there's been some tender moments between those clean white hotel sheets. Some absolutely terrible ones as well, but usually on my own with pornography and incontinence.

The tender scenes where love has fluttered her little yellow wings and slutfreak is transformed from venereal whore bitch cunt who should not be doing this with a man old enough to be her father, into fresh-faced virgin French girl. I shit you not my brothers and sisters, it can, and does happen. Almost entirely, for me anyway, with French women. It's the accent, corny I know, but I get mahogany just listening to them talk about what they want for breakfast. And a fine low centre of gravity Nip chick, they never fail to get my balls all confused, sending chemicals to my head, saying I'm in love. You think all this sex god shagging shit is easy?

That's what I used to think, till I noticed all these little chips missing from my heart.

The bitches were taking pieces from me when I slept, creeping into my soul, hacking off a chunk and then fucking off, back to their normal lives, boyfriends, husbands, babies. And I was stuck on that infernal highway, rocking and rocking and rocking.

I hadn't learned how to roll.

Learning to roll is a skill that takes fucking years of the hardest, most serious, liver-hardening, brain-stomping, soul-shredding rocking of all to crack. It's the nearest we men of the black leather church ever get to any form of enlightenment, learning to roll.

Like saying I think I've had enough.

Poor old Kurt, stupid cunt, he never learnt how to roll.

THE BOX

When I consider some of the ludicrous things involving Gimpo over these past dangerous years, I am swamped by an avalanche of such overwhelming disbelief that I almost start wheezing myself into an asthma attack. And I don't even have asthma.

It must have been somewhere around November.

Gimpo had fireworks.

Now anyone who knows Gimpo, knows that the combination of those two elements, the Gimp and fireworks – well, I think you know what I mean.

We were rehearsing at Fat-Arsed Frank's rehearsal rooms in King's Cross – I don't know why. We could rehearse for a year and we would still make the same musical fuck-ups, and I would never be able to remember even half the lyrics even if we rehearsed for ten fucking years.

But I suppose it was preferable to getting bedshitting drunk and lying around tugging in your own diarrhoea, some lazy punk rock bitch with a sore arse, farting and snoring with alcohol poisoning laying beside you.

More than any of his other duties Gimpo was supposed to keep us amused, if he didn't we would start doing really stupid shit, like kidnapping groupies and torturing them. We didn't have a problem with it, but Balfe, our sour faced, curmudgeonly manager would bust a gut when he caught us gaffa taping some teenage slagbag to the wall and setting her hair on fire.

He was such a wimp sometimes. We always let them go at the end, what was his fucking problem? Such a hypocrite as well, he had no moralistic qualms about the punk rock bitch bumming, even spearing a couple of them himself once after one or two backstage beers. They did look cute though. Gaffa taped to the wall, with just their cute little fifteen-year-old punk rock arses peeking through the silvery bandages.

So we're going through our mistakes for the nine millionth time when the door opens, and there he is with that smile that we all knew went hand in hand with seriously demented Gimpo mischief. He had a big bag with him.

Cobalt was fumbling his way through some pointless guitar solo, grinding away like some public masturbator mashing it big style in front of the local girls' school when the rocket missed his gurning head by about an inch, the jumping crackers were banging and cracking all over the floor.

Gimpo had just spent half the band's float on fireworks. Excellent.

MARK MANNING

Money well spent, we all agreed.

We had a great couple of hours doing as many illegal and dangerous things as even an eight-year-old would have to have tried hard to beat. If you've never seen a cat with a whole bunch of jumping crackers tied to its tail, and a banger stuffed up its arse, my friend, you have not lived.

When all the bangers, airbombs and rockets had nearly started the second fire of London and we were down to our last two rockets, which the Gimp lit in his hands and aimed at a passing pregnant woman, a sense of disappointment and ennui slid over us.

Fire. We wanted more fire. We wanted *lots* more fire.

The boy did good, ten minutes later he's back on the scene with enough lighter fuel to light the fags of all of China for the next twenty-eight years. Butane, liquid, the whole fucking lot, and a big box of party poppers.

After a few fire dances, setting fire to our pants and running around in the dark, laughing like insane people, things hitched up a notch.

Gimpo had found The Box.

I don't know where, not that it matters, it was a big brown cardboard one, from a fridge or something. The tasty little pyromaniac was buggering around with it, cutting a small hole at the bottom into which he inserted one of those party poppers. We stood around intrigued. When Gimpo shows any sort of concerted effort the results were usually of a destructive and amusing nature. It was Gimpo who thought of gaffa taping groupies to the wall before we gang raped them. He was clever that way. I'll never forget the time when we came off stage at some bog or another and the Gimps had prepared a little surprise for us. Some poor girl gaffa taped face down on the floor with just her arse peering through the silver plastic bonds. I had the piss ripped out of me for weeks because I wouldn't bugger the arse.

She wasn't a fifteen-year-old punk rock bitch; I was getting weird, perverted. I could only fuck fifteen-year-old punk rock bitches. "A fucking bird's arse is a fucking bird's arse," said Kid Chaos, stabbing the screaming girl's blart socket.

I knew he was right.

"You're turning into a fucking weirdo," said the Gimp. Bastards.

Anyway, after bollocking around with the party popper he started emptying entire cans of butane gas into the cardboard box; it must have been the one thing he learned from school chemistry lessons, that butane was heavier

than air.

To say that the little pyromaniacal prank was anything less than spectacular would be lying.

We herded behind the amps and peered nervously over them as king firebug lay on his belly, covered his face, and stretching his hand at arm's length pulled the party popper. BOOM! It was fantastic, a huge blast of flames blew out of the cardboard box and scorched the ceiling. Some vacuum, gas, science thing blasting the heavy rehearsal room door almost off its hinges. Of course we wanted more. "Again Gimpo, with the lights out!" BOOM!

We were hysterical, like a bunch of overexcited drag queens. Inevitably we wanted more, more fire, more danger – danger to Gimpo of course, not to our cowardly selves. "Hold the box, hold the box!" we chanted, like we were seven years old and we were in the school playground egging on the school daredevil. Which, I guess is what it was really, when I think about it.

"Put more gas in it Gimps you fucking poof!" I shouted.

"Yeah Gimps, you're boring," egged on the Stargazer, knowing exactly which buttons to press to take the Gimp to the edge of whatever demented ledge he was dancing on that week.

Pyro boy filled the cardboard box with enough gas to wipe out a whole synagogue and heaved it onto his shoulders. Me and the rest of the girls hid behind the amps, I was sure Gimps was going to blast himself out of existence.

He pulled the party popper, and the box, like a fucking bazooka, flame thrower, bomb shit, blasted out apocalyptic flames, knocking our kamikaze mongoloid tour manager flat on his arse.

Of course we wanted more. The fucker wasn't dead or suffering third degree burns yet. Just bald, without any eyebrows – the back blast had burnt all his hair off.

"In the box! In the box!" we chanted, Lord of the Flies vibe descending down big time on our subnormal little piggy.

The thing one always has to remember about Gimpo and his kind is they cannot decline a dare, the thought of even being thought of as a girl is terrifying to them. It took a bit of goading: "God you're so boring these days Gimpo."

"Have you been taking female hormones or something Gimpeena?"

"Nice bra Gimps, did you knit it yourself?"

MARK MANNING

"The real Gimps would have jumped straight in the box, must be his new boyfriend or something."

Gimpo, stoked to the limit by these childish taunts, eyes bulging, blue and mad, stormed out of the rehearsal room. We laughed evilly at our merciless taunting of danger boy, thinking he'd bottled it and gone home.

We should have known better.

Five minutes later, the door slams open and there he is, Lord Pyro, with ten cans of butane and a fire extinguisher. "Right!" he shouted. "If I'm on fire, just point this fucker at me, and put me out, you bunch of women!"

After he'd sprayed the last of the cans of butane into that dreadful box I started getting really worried. Tour managers don't come cheap, and Gimpo was cheap.

The room had a sort of reverential silence; was the mad firebald fucking bastard really going to stand in that box full of ten cans of butane and ignite? He was.

We cowered behind the drum kit as Gimpo prepared to become charcoal kebab boy.

He carefully adjusted his balaclava, struck the match, and KABOOM! It was truly spectacular, I couldn't believe he'd really done it. I can still remember his insane sooty grin beaming out from the fireball which literally blew the door off its hinges and toasted Slam's snaredrum.

Of course hero fireboy had to go and ruin his hour of glory by performing a little victory fire dance, jigging around and pouring liquid lighter fuel all over his pants, setting them alight as he did his mental little jig. Somehow the fumes penetrated his pants and an inflammable gas pocket built up and nearly burnt his cock off. He started screaming and pulling his pants down, all his bollocks and pube stuff flaming away like a fire in a sausage shop. Quick-thinking Slam sprayed the flaming genitalia with the fire extinguisher, obviously using far more than nescessary. Gimps tried to run out of the rehearsal room covered in foam, screaming, and tripped over his fiery jeans, concussing himself against the studio wall.

He was only in hospital a couple of days, second degree burns of the buggery sausage and minor head injuries.

How we laughed and laughed.

Rock and roll friends, it wasn't all bad.

OH GOD, ONE OF THE TUGGERS IS TRYING TO TALK TO ME

Salzburg. Birth place of Mozart. One of the most beautiful cities in the world. Its winding cobbled streets full of Alpine pleasures. A place so beautiful one of the most romantic and sugar-laden films of the twentieth century was filmed there.

The Sound Of Music.

The film's saccharine artificiality and technicolour beauty has more or less made its theme music the homosexual community's national anthem.

Even behind the chocolate box beauty and clean air of the place it really is breath-taking. The pearl of Austria's crown.

And what did we do in Salzburg?

We found the tug shop.

Maybe he was missing his wife or something, but Tex, man, he nearly outdid himself. We were wandering around its car-free cobbled streets, sampling the delightful pastries and chocolates, stopping for the odd five pints of clear Austrian beer, took a ride on the cablecar up to the delightful restaurant, where we farted and drank another five pints of clear cool, beautiful lager. We were there for a couple of days, so our mood was relaxed.

We cabled down and headed back to the bus and then like some kind of perverted carrier pigeon that always finds its way home, the Mexican wanking boy, through some undocumented porno skill, had homed in on the tiny little tug shop hidden down a narrow alley.

Tug cabins, written in felt tip on a piece of pink cardboard in the window of what looked like a hairdressing shop.

Down the worn carpeted stairs we trudged, tumescently troubled.

As tug shops go, it was pretty run of the mill. Anal torture, gaffa tape bondage, the usual tug magazine staples. There were a few cabins where for a couple of coins you could batter yourself into oblivion for a while, watching those porno gymnasts go through their spermy repertoire of shagging, blowing and bumming. It was still early morning, about ten o'clock or so, so I wasn't really in the mood for any serious spam-strangling. Cobalt, me and Robbie checked out a couple of cabins but decided we would rather drink beer till we passed out. Tex seemed extraordinarily tuggish, so we left him to

MARK MANNING

it.

The sun was going down as we all slid in and out of consciousness in a bar that had somehow trapped us. Tex kept coming and going, drinking beer, looking weird.

"Where the fuck do you keep going man?" I asked the twitchy wanker.

"That fucking tug shop man, have you checked all the movies those cats are playing down there?" he said, smoking nervously.

"Yeah man, usual spank vids, nothing special," I replied carefully, trying to make sure that the words of my sentence came out in the right order; I was pretty drunk.

"Must be me man, I been down there six times today, my fucking hard-on, it just won't go away."

I spied a cruel little joke somewhere amongst the bass-playing burrito boy's temporary satyriasis (that's like brainy talk for wankdisease). "Fuck it yeah man, I could do with a quick tug, let's go."

My plan wasn't quite focused but I knew that there was an excellent way to humiliate and laugh at old Texy boy's quandary somewhere in that blur-fisted world.

It didn't take long. In the tug shop, a girl so plain, bordering on ugly sat at the desk giving the tuggers change so they could feed the porno machines until their ballbags were drained. Bingo.

"Tex man, you know that chick that does the change thing, don't you think she's kind of cute in a weird kind of way?" I said as we browsed the racks of *Bumhole Fever* magazine and *Gynaecological Nightmare Monthly*.

Tex took furtive looks at the four-eyed, semi-mongoloid freak dishing out the tug money. Obviously his judgement was way in the stratosphere, I could see him somehow, through some tuggish überpower, transforming tug-features into Cindy Crawford.

"Yeah man, I didn't notice before, but you're kind of right," said tugboy. This was his seventh visit, man was he on a tug trip or what?

"Hey honey," Wankboy said to the startled tug lady. "I'm kinda like in a rock band shit, we're playing in town tonight, wanna come along?"

The poor girl. One of the tuggers was talking to her, one that had been in seven times that day. Obviously she was terrified. "Papa!" she screamed. "The tuggers are talking to me!"

"Yeah JuJus, and erm, a coke," said Travis Texy boy. Man it was pure *Taxi*

Driver, the scene were Travis Bickle tries a little small talk with the porn cinema chick. I laughed and laughed so much I shat my pants.
Needless to say, Tuggerella didn't come to the gig.

Cobalt Stargazer

Gladiator, scourge of the fretboard,
singeing the atmosphere with
napalm licks
Eyes search Heaven, soul cruises
the gutter, Ramrod Stargazer on
latex marathon
Love is blind, Cobalt wears shades
Bacon digit, grunge king
Franky Bootstomper with hedge-
hogs writhing in his Y-fronts
Silver tongue lolls lasciviously on
alcohol slack jaw
Baron Bullshit believes in his
carpet
Cobalt in a coma fights Jack D and
loses with vomit spectaculars
Furnace in his trousers and a fire-
proof wallet
Cobalt loves his money but hates
spending it

SEX AND SHIT AND ROCK AND ROLL

Rock and roll, touring and completely depraved pornography go together like brussels sprouts and cream.

Occasionally at some haunted motel – Ed Gein's transvestite ghost mother drifting through the walls, wandering lone serial killers masturbating in icy air conditioned rooms – you'd occasionally come across other tour-fried British bands.

In these strange forgotten places, isolated amongst the tumbleweed and deserts of the South-Westerly states of America, you'd be drinking in the dusty bar, necking tequila after tequila for long slow hours, mumbling increasingly slurred inanities before you realised that the greasy-haired wreck of a human being, black t-shirt covered in sperm stains, sitting next to you wasn't your bass guitarist at all, but some guy from the Mission.

Or any other collection of black leather degenerates sodomising groupies and shredding their livers around the terrifying tornado of moronic synapse that is America.

This in itself is testament to how the grinding similarity of these stints in the goldmines of Sodom were driving us fucked-up minstrels, far from home, ever lower into a maelstrom of megalithic filth.

Industrial strength cocaine flying around spermy rooms, sparking cacophonous rackets of bawling retardology. Every man in the room a genius with some mind-blowingly profound observation about the correct etiquette for the buggering of punk rock bitches.

Filthy, Mexican heroin cut with dried pig blood, and dried-out beaner turds. Just about every other evil chemical and gene-twisted herb hummed like evil electricity, oscillating your ragged serotonin levels rapidly between high and low, high and very low, high and even lower, high and suicidal.

Super weird, peyote, mescal shit that got you so screwed up you weren't even high or low, but flapping your fried turkey wings in some sideways fucked up dimension where there weren't even any words, in English anyway, to describe the way you were free falling out of sanity and into something even further out than madness. A place in overspace and supertime it was so mindfucking far H.P. Lovecraft out, it had to be real.

Maybe those peyote-freak shaman Indian dudes had some way of describing this eyeball tangling, inside out, hellweird place, but I sure fucking didn't.

FUCKED BY ROCK

I was so lost, I found it completely normal to watch some unwashed, scabby stranger tying up his skeleton-bone arm with a belt and squirting blood out of his filthy works in slow motion all across the motel walls.

Takeaway groupies, just call them up and they're delivered like pizza, their gorgonzola buckets even looking and smelling like pizza, all manner of hideous foot and cunt diseases dribbling down their legs, normal, all bands do it.

The hellish party that had been rolling for months reached another peak. Punk rock bitches would be taken out of their boxes, water thrown on their faces to wake them out of their drug torpor before they were buggered savagely in motel corridors and then thrown out into the cold desert night to fend for themselves amongst the coyotes and wandering, feral roadies, who'd missed the tour bus and had turned completely wild, scavenging around motel dustbins for burgers and OD'd groupies.

But most treasured and competitively coveted at these hobo conventions were the vids that were eagerly exchanged. What beauts had our fellow troubadours brought back from that black capital of pornographic Dogshit Earth, Mother Deutchsland?

These videos were never really used for tugging, well apart from the Gimp, who as I have mentioned on many an occasion had excused himself through some private negotiation with the Devil from being a part of the human race.

It was somewhere around either the Reeperbahn or Amsterdam.

The whores, drugs and general smells of KY and anus-gargling, transvestite prostitutes in Bela Lugosi drag wafting on the balmy summer air always confused me.

Perverts all look alike to me.

I was in the back lounge with the Count, Europe always brought out the undead in the Stargazer, never leaving his bunk till after dark, even in Rome, one of the most beautiful cities in the world.

All cities were the same to the Count.

Cattlemarkets.

Brimful of gash. Fuck the architecture it was the minge that the Count was interested in. Lapping up that menstrual blood feeding his libidic vampire soul, energizing the dark Satanic power of his most treasured guitar, the Sleazegrinder.

MARK MANNING

Where was I? Ah yes, the back lounge watching another vile video, some woman stuffing eels up her cunt, the usual, pretty average stuff. Some deranged woman with surgical instruments, screws and stretchy metal things pulling her bumhole so far apart it made me wince. God you could fit your fucking head up there, and of course some bald-headed retarded looking guy wearing swimming goggles did.

Who were these people? What had this to do with sex? Like making babies and stuff. To be quite honest it all seriously confused me, but it was fascinating all the same.

How did German people get to be so grossly perverted, I mean you could buy this stuff in regular grocery stores, along with your cheeses and Bratwürst.

It had to have to something to do with all that Nazi shit, I mean a lot of those fuckers were still alive, especially in Munich.

Especially in Munich.

All that self-loathing and secret desire to rise again and finish those fucking chicken soup-swilling bastards off completely. It must have gone all curdled and shitted up in the collective horrorshow of those sausage munchers' national psyche.

"Shit, I'm fucking bored of all this animal fucking tug!" said the Gimp, clicking off the TV.

"Oi you cunt, I was fucking watching that, the blood sausage and the ferret were on next!" shouted Cobalt.

"Yeah you cunt, fucking leave it, I still can't work out how that ferret goes in her cunt and comes out of her arse," I added, genuinely mystified by this gynaecological mystery.

I'd even been studying Cobalt's *Grays Anatomy*. It seemed impossible.

"Maybe she does cocaine in her fanny and she's burnt a hole from her cunt tube into her arse tube, like cokeheads do with their nose," said Cobalt.

"Why the fuck would she want to do that?" I replied perplexed.

"Why the fuck would she want to put a fucking rat up her fucking bucket!" laughed the Stargazer.

"Yeah, hmm, you're right, it's a ferret though isn't it, they're like really wriggly, maybe it goes up into her intestines and wriggles around and finds her buggery chute," I muttered, mystified. "Turn it back on Gimp, I need to know how that fucking ferret gets out of her arse when it goes up her fucking cunt, it's physically impossible," I ordered.

"For fuck's sake, are you thick or something?" answered the Gimp, exasperated. "It's a fucking trick innit, like David Copperfield or something, she's probably got a mirror up there or something," said the porno master.

"Or it could be trick photography," added the inspired Stargazer; we were definitely homing in on the answer to this perplexing porno puzzle.

"Of course, fucking hell I must be losing it, they probably just stop the camera and get the ferret out and stuff it up her arse, then film it coming out, fucking hell man, what a fucking porno chump," I said, feeling dumb.

"Alright, Sherlock porno fucking Holmes, come on, now you've worked out Frieda's little bumhole trick, I've found a fucking unbelievable tug shop, hidden away down some shitty little ginnel," shouted the main man of wanking.

If Gimpo said he had found a good one there was more than an odds-on chance it was gruesome beyond all belief. The Gimp took his entertainment duties seriously.

Cobalt put on some sunblock – there was still a little sun setting in the west, and Cobalt had convinced himself that he would burst into flames should the sunlight touch his undead flesh. As he pulled on his leather pervert gloves we followed our porn piper out into that square acre of base desire. Excited at the thought of discovering some new horror porn with which to wile away those rolling miles of drugs, buggery and ennui.

The descent into the warren of stinking litter-strewn streets was like travelling deeper and deeper into another world. There were canals all over the place, so I guessed it must have been Amsterdam.

I was getting quite excited, despite the fact that I was more of a Reeperbahn man myself. I liked the Teutonic efficiency, how even within the realms of sexual and moral insanity, order prevailed.

How on one side of the bahn there was all the sexual insanity shops and on the other side all the violence shops huddled together, like a fruggle of paedophiles, selling cool-looking guns, swords, daggers, knives, axes and all other kinds of sharp evil raping things.

You could even get over-the-counter Rohypnol.

My favourite recreational drug.

But for some reason I got a sneaking feeling, slithering around in my underpants like a dying trout, that old Gimpy might have made another wankish little breakthrough in our escalating world of ultra-depravity.

MARK MANNING

I wasn't wrong.

The air seemed to become more foetid, the canals narrower, more like open sewers, the stagnant water covered with a slimy blanket of rotting condoms. The small alleyways, narrower and narrower making it difficult to pass any faecal pervert shuffling from the other direction.

In the dark doorways, smoking cigarettes and smelling of mint and blowjobs were the poor man's whores. Transvestites in PVC, goth nightmare drag who would suck you off or let you bum them for less than half the price of a female whore. If you used your imagination I guess it was possible that you could believe that they were real sluts.

But live buggery and cocksucking, we were sorted for that with our punk rock bitches and regular groupie hornsmokers. It was the tug we were interested in.

The way Gimpo had got all excited I reckoned he'd found some specialist chicken tug, little Brazilian kids getting funky with their uncles and aunties. That would have been a pleasant surprise compared to what the rotten Mancunian masturbator had located on his gruesome scout into the white fish-belly sliminess of that stained and imperfect thing, the human soul.

There it was lurking under a blue light, a small blacked-out window with a small badly chipped brown wooden door. There were no signs or anything, no lurid pictures of women being raped and forced to suck on men's bumholes through their underpants. No freaks suspended from the light fittings by their ballbags, heads in leather masks with those weird billiard ball things stuck in their mouths.

No horrible lifelike-looking severed fourteen-inch dicks.

No boxes of inflatable choirgirl dolls, all of them singing in perfect harmony that blorping hymn to hornsmoking.

No handcuffs, jars of Bum OK snake oil. No tanks full of live eels or dirty cages full of small wriggling rodents.

So how Gimpo had known that this innocuous-looking shop front contained what it did I have no idea. I guess he must have developed a nose for these things. He knocked on the door grinning and turning to us. "Here we go lads," he said, that icey blue twinkle in his tugger's eye. "Willy Wanker's choc factory." He laughed as the noise of several locks and bolts being thrown came from the other side of the door. I groaned inwardly, I had a horrible feeling that I knew what this sewage-surfing pud-puller had located during

his his greasy, fisty rambles.

I was right. A fucking choc shop.

A horror parlour of everything coprographic.

Jesus fucking Christ, you could almost smell the stuff.

Thousands and thousands of videos of people shitting all over each other, eating the fucking stuff, smearing it all over each other like melted chocolate. Black chicks, Chinky birds, Deutsche girls, always lots of Deutsche girls. Asian women, even goddamn Lappish women, dumping away happily.

Nearly all the men without exception except for a few Downs Syndrome type-looking guys appeared to be big fat, spotty-arsed Germans.

It must be a national fucking sport or something. Have you ever seen those German khazis? The ones with the shelves, which catches the shite before it hits the water so you can have a poke around with it.

Gimpo was in his element. "Fucking hell, look at this!" the turd-fancier shouted. He'd found a section which was divided into dietary sections, listing the food that each dumper had eaten for the fortnight before the filming had begun; the mind boggled. Cabbage and liver, it would seem produced a diarrhoea shite pissing out of fat Fritz's arse like projectile vomiting. Boiled eggs and chocolate, enabled the Teutonic turd warriors to heave mighty brown boulders out through stretched ring pieces.

Kheema curry and vindaloo ingestation, produced a lumpy diarrhoetic paste not as liquid as the cabbage and liver. The picture on the vid showed a rosy-cheeked teenage girl smearing her tits with shit that looked like the molten discharge of a smack-addled turkey. The variations seemed endless.

I noticed that Cobalt had turned an even paler shade of puce than his ordinarily bloodless shade of undead white, and his knees were going.

It was obviously all too much for him, he was about to faint. I helped my friend to his feet and took him to the entrance, much to the amusement of scatboy who was pissing his pants with laughter; he had succeeded in wimping us out.

Maybe the battle Gimpo, but not the campaign, I thought to myself evilly as I led the ill guitarist to the door. I paused at the doorway and addressed the guy sat by the till. The guy was Downs Syndrome. Downs Syndrome and German. "There's fucking something fucking wrong with you mate," I said as I opened the door. "Ja," he laughed, obviously not understanding a word I was saying, "Ja? Ha, ha, is good ja?" he said, pointing to a monitor of some projectile squitting. "TTHHHRRRPPP!" he raspberried in his own little unterkraut world.

"Ha, ha,ha, ffrrrttt!" He laughed again, he had his stumpy little subnormal dick out and was bashing away enthusiastically. I shook my head and stepped outside. Cobalt immediately hurled all down his black leather Dracula trousers.

The sewerish air smelled fresh after the arsegrease stench of Willy's terrible factory.

We made our way back to the bus to watch some ordinary eels for pleasure and anal torture vids.

Gimpo, he truly was a fucking pervert, Jesus.

But this faecal incident didn't end there, oh no my brothers and sisters, it got fucking worse, as you shall soon see.

We were rewinding the tape, playing it in slow motion trying to see any evidence of discontinuity in the ferret video. But no fucking way, it's a steady hand-held shot, the ferret covered in what appears to be Bum OK snake oil slithers up the depraved red-headed pervert woman's snatch and ten seconds later covered in black shite comes wriggling out of her arse like an over-animated turd with a life of its own. How the fuck does she do it?

"It's got to be a trick," said Cobalt with a furrowed brow. "It's a physical impossibility," he added, thumbing through his *Grays Anatomy*.

"Maybe she's had it done surgically," I suggested, a brainwave of tuggology hitting me like a jizz oyster under the chin after a week-long holiday from the bashing.

"What do you mean? Why on earth would anyone want to have a ferret tunnel burrowed into her bear trap?" said Cobalt, looking even more confused, this fucking ferret thing was really getting to him.

"Well, think about it right," I began to explain. "You know like those American stripper women with the monster 77" double FF tits have those ridiculous silicon implants, to do loads of photos, films and all that shit, dancing all over America, running their own fan clubs and all of that shit yeah?" I explained. "They make a fucking couple of mill, then have the silicon taken out and settle down to a normal life with lots of pets," I added, more confidently.

"Well no, I didn't actually, but carry on." I think Cobalt was getting the

picture.

"Well there must be a lot of money to be made from these weird animal burrowing films," I continued earnestly, warming to my theory.

"You think so?" said Cobalt, looking worried.

"Yeah man, porno's like a drug, the tuggers start off with the usual shagging and fisting, arse-shagging stuff, then they need more and more filth, they're like junkies – they have to keep upping the dosage, the filth factor, to get any result. And just think how many hardcore tuggers there are in Germany, where porno's been legal for over thirty years." My reasoning was working on the undead guitarist. "So Miss fuckin Zoo-Fanny woman here, has a hole from her cunt to her arse done by some Brazilian surgeon so she can make these sort of films, makes a fucking fortune from sticking wriggly animals into her cunt, jack russells, moles and what have you, naturally inquisitive burrowing animals, retires after making a fucking bomb then has the hole sewn up and settles down to raise a family with her husband. That's got to be it," I added.

But before he could reply, our hearts dropped as old devil fist Gimpo came running up the stairs with a plastic bag with the choc factory label on it

"Oh shit," groaned Cobalt. Indeed, I almost added.

There was no way Gimpo was going to win on this. He'd already humiliated Cobalt in the shop by causing him to faint. Our manly honour was at stake. We felt safer somehow in the safety of the back lounge, almost prepared for whatever scatological *guignol* our masturbating monster of a tour manager had in his fetid little bag. The cunt had ambushed us at Willy's, had us all puking in the tug booths, but back in the womb-like safety of the tourbus we soon turned the tables on wankgnome by simply playing the tapes back-wards.

As we had already learned, this negates the horror of any horror porn.

Gimpo's face dropped when he realised that we were no longer grossed out by his little cartoon.

Nice try Gimp, but you'll have to try harder next time.

Note to bands with horrible tour managers: see CHOC VID on page 175 for a further explanation of this technique.

TUGGERS AND TOREROS
A TRUE STORY OF THE WEST

Well, almost true. It depends on whether you believe in the realities of hallucination and delirium.

Me, I can't tell the difference any more.

The people of western countries live their lives beneath frail illusions that are different yet fundamentaly the same.

Culture, Language and Religion are merely different shades of the same dream.

The one we call civilization.

And it is as fragile as a sparrow's bones.

True war, as Carl von Clausewitz, the military theorist tells us, is the only thing that shows us as we really are.

Beasts.

And this is why we need these illusions.

Illusions that have evolved over the years, with laws and enforcers of laws to sustain them.

Governments, armies, judges, police officers.

Not so long ago, Westerners believed that certain human beings were animals and bought and sold them to work in cotton fields and sugar plantations.

In a society like this, it is hard for those people of a sensitive and intelligent nature to stay sane. Surrounded on all flanks by the contented and the deluded, who sunbathe beneath satellites of cynical lies and twisted half truths concocted by the rich and powerful.

The cosmosodomistic order of the black gas is what it is called.

Globalistic capitalism is the order's own pathetic spin.

Evil bastards that utilise the subliminal and the subtextual in every arm of their vast blatantly invisible campaigns, through banal advertising and the most arcane aristocratic rituals designed to mind-rape us dopes down here in the cash sludge to covet things that we don't need, and pay for them with money that we don't have.

Credit is its black gas name.

Indentured slavery its real one.

But this illusion is weakening, its hull creaking beneath the pressure being

applied by the young. Who are slowly wising up, seeing through the strategies of the cosmosodomistic conspirators. Turning the mechanics of this black gas back on itself. The newly computer literate and disenfranchised. How long before we raise the standard of a new cyber Che. An icon that speaks to the melting ice chip hearts of their inbred offspring.

War, children. It's just a chip away, just a byte away.

Well that's a weird introduction to an even weirder tale.

And who can say that the illusion Tex and myself developed wasn't as real as all the above? We merely refocused reality for a while. Replaced one illusion with a homegrown one. But out there in the antipodes of the mind's darkest corners, shit can get pretty heavy *hombre*, as you will see.

Of course it all revolved around the ridiculous amounts of drugs and alcohol we were guzzling, smoking, injecting and snorting. And yet?

Madrid, the start of the bullfight season; we were making a record there, it was cheap. Tex and myself got our parts done real quick so we had plenty of time to go mad under that Spanish sun. Our jokes took on a life of their own and we started to really believe them.

We thought we were in a place called Tugtown and the dread sheriff of Tugtown was after us, we had committed some terrible crime and there was a reward on our heads, dead or alive. And that mean old sheriff... "Hey man, you don' wanna fock with heem, he's bad man.... you know what I am saying homes."

I'll try and tell you what happened to get us into this pitiful state.

Of course those two bad best friends cocaine Jack and Dick whiskey played an important part in this Spanish insanity, but our overstimulated imaginations and the mind blowing level of intensity that the locals put into their partying helped lubricate us along that broken glass headfuck big time. Scotchy B, the producer and engineer asked us immediately on our arrival if we fancied seeing some live tug. We weren't exactly sure what he meant, but it sounded intriuging to say the least.

The pervert producer took us on a long walk through the narrow and twisting back alleys across the central square and once more into an even more convoluted warren of dingy, narrow back alleys. The whores were out, and the streets had that tuggish vibe that only us master tuggers can feel. I was right, as we turned around another corner, Scotchy's eyes lit up, literally, reflecting the flashing neon. It was pretty impressive to say the least: EL

the brotherhood of tug
"meet my libido – he's a psycho"

FUCKERAMA flashed the neon sign. It looked huge, even bigger than that other European hypermarket of masturbation, the SEXODROME in Paris. "Fucking hell," said Tex, a dirty smile lighting up his face.

"What the fuck is this place man?" he said.

"It's the Vatican of wanking, Homeboy," said old Scotchy, the horny-fisted record producer.

I noticed a few pale-faced guys skulking out through the revolving doors, they had that drained look about them, fully-committed tuggers, heavy eyelids, shifty, brown paper bags hugged close to their chests, ill from all that tugging.

Inside it was the usual story, hundreds of thousands of videos and magazines, *Buggery Apocalypse, Shit Sluts Of Sweden, Doctor My Arse Hurts*, all the classics were there.

But it wasn't the videos we'd come to see, it was the live tug we were here for. Scotchy hadn't exactly told us what he meant by live tug, wanted to keep it as a surprise. We walked down into the darkened low ceilinged corridor, ordinary tug cabins on either side – you could hear the muffled moaning and cheesy music as some Spanish wanker polished his pork whilst watching the short, daft little videos of women having it off with orangutans and stuff.

There was this deafening techno music booming away, with some Tugger DJ speaking in a submarine creepy Spanish voice: "Sexy, sexy, sexy, sexy, sexy, sexuaaallllhy! Numero uno!" He kept calling out numbers, it sounded quite sinister, dripping reverb all over the fucking place. "Sexy, sexy sexy, sexuaaaallly," the disembodied voice kept saying. It was scary, I felt like we'd wandered into one of Dante's lost circles of Hell.

We eventually arrived at a large circular room of doors.

Our pale, weak-looking tug brothers shifted around avoiding eye contact, they all seemed to be in some kind of masturbatory trance, glazed expressions, eyes looking at some invisible horizon.

The voice boomed out again making me jump. "Sexy, sexy, sexy sexuaaallly! Numero dias!" A couple of the skulking tuggers ran to the circle of doors when Sexy Sexy had called out the number.

Scotchy explained. There were pictures of naked girls on the walls, each with a number and a name. "When Sexy Sexy calls out the number that means she's in there buggering around sticking her arse in your face and stuff, doing the wanking dancing," said Wanky B.

MARK MANNING

"Eugh!" Cobalt replied. "It sounds horrible." Old Texy didn't think it sounded horrible, the tugger's twinkle in his eyes and the big fat smile told you that he quite liked the idea of one of these wanking dancing chicks stuffing her tin can in his face.

It seemed pretty good to me too. Me and Tex went over to see the pictures, there wasn't much in it, they all had big tits and too much make-up on. "Fuck it man, I'm going in now, I ain't seen any decent wanking dancing since I left LA," said the sophisticated Mexican bass player. "Me too," I said trying to find an empty cabin. Cobalt, feigning resignation, had found an empty booth and slid in furtively, an eel swimming in shifty swarfega. Scotchy was already in there bashing for Britain. I closed the door behind me and put in my coins and a one-foot-square peephole opened and there she was, the live tug, squirming around and bending over showing her arse and stuff. I was just about to get into some violent spam-strangling when my dick collapsed faster than diarrhoea. Over on the other side of the circular bed thing I could see Tex, a cigarette in the side of his mouth, one eye closed pulling these horrible contorted tugging faces. Oh my God! There was Cobalt gurning away, his shoulder bopping away at top speed, like he's changing gear at fucking Le Mans or something, Schumacher grinding up his Mach 3 arse. And Scotchy B, battering away, pulling Evil Dead faces. I shot out of the booth immediately. No way could I hurl a bollock oyster with those ugly bastards hammering away, grimacing like something from *Bashwank Apocalypse 47*, whatever that was.

Fuck me. I wondered if I looked like that when I was smacking spanky, God I hoped not. I went over to study the gallery of live tug sluts. Actually some of them weren't that bad, Seafood Sally, she was kind of fuckable, as was Spermelina Pissflaps, though Julie Bumhole was a bit of a dog. I eventually decided that Quimly Divine was the best of the bunch, although Suzy Ringslinger came a close, tin can, second.

Out came my fellow tuggers. I told them what had happened, I couldn't understand why none of them had seen me or all the other indigenous tuggers.

"Shit man," said Tex in his funny Mexican voice, "I was focused on the gash man, didn't even notice any of the native tuggers." Cobalt and Scotchy said the same, Cobalt even denied having a tug at all, well what the fuck was he doing in there, some little Irish jig or something. "Shit man, I'm gonna go in

again, look they got a bar over there."

They did as well. That was probably the strangest thing of all, there in that church of the five-fingered martyr. What were you supposed to do? Have a little drink with your fellow masturbators, chat pleasantly to fellow wankers while your nads refilled.

I mean tugging's a kind of solo thing, we were the only pack wankers in there, all the other sexual lepers were on their own. Scurrying around furtively or waiting by the circular doors until their favourite live tugbird's name and number was called.

Sexy Sexy was reverberating again. "Sexy, sexy sexuaaaallo," he boomed like some voodoo porno dragon from the dark side of the moon, the soup dragons' hideeously deformed, sexually insane, five-knuckle bareback clanging cousin. "SEXUAAAAAHLLLO!!!" he repeated again louder. It sounded like some sort of hellish muzzein, "SEXUAAAAAHAHALO! SEXY, SEXY SEXY!" Calling the faithful jizz-whackers to their one-handed prayers. Bending over and farting in each other's faces. All praise to Tuggah! There was a stampede towards the tugging circle, indigenous tuggers emerging from everywhere, cabin doors slamming, two tuggers burst out of the same video cabin and literally ran down the corridor, they were coming from all over the fucking place, out of the floors, leaping over balconies pulling anxiously at all the door handles, desperately trying to find an empty one. "What the fuck did Sexy Sexy just say?" I wanted to know.

"Something about a casa, full house kind of thing, I'm not sure," said Tex. Old Scotchy, he fucking knew alright.

"It's when all the wanking dancers come out together, and do the lesbo stuff."

"What all twenty of them at once?" said the Mexican fist artist. "I'm definitely staying here for another go then," he said draining his beer and ordering another. "How long before they do it again?"

"Oh about every hour or so. There's private live tug rooms as well," added the serious old basher, Scotchy B. "It's a small cubicle with a sheet of glass and a telephone, so you can tell her what to do and stuff."

"What do you mean?" I asked, this sounded interesting, one-to-one tugging, why don't we have this shit in England I wondered.

"Yeah, she comes into the room with a little bag of dildos and stuff, and you talk to her on the phone, tell her what to do, bend over stick that pink one up your arse, put more swarfega on your tits, that sort of stuff," said ol' pervy

MARK MANNING

B.

"What and she can see you, choking Kojak and pulling weird faces?" I said intrigued.

"Hey man, I think I'm gonna go there when my balls are full again, how much is it man?" said Tex, feeling his balls, willing them to fill up faster.

It was almost the same amount as a hooker, so Tex boy waited for the full house number again. "Sexy, Sexy Sexy SEXUAAAAHHAAHAAHAAHALO! Casa completa!" This time he sounded like fucking Tarzan. "SEXY SEXY SEXUUUAAHAAHAAHAAHAHAAHLLLO!" Tuggers swinging down on vines, elephants screaming as demented perverts stuck their heads up the pachyderms' ambushed arseholes, sort of reversed pet shop boy, Richard Gere, jungleboy shit, if you get my drift.

We raced into the wanking scrum and managed to get a cabin each. I tried not to see my tugging friends and just focused on the lesbo action, but my attention slipped and I found myself looking at Tex's face, God it was horrible.

All contorted, his tongue squeezing out from a jawlock expression. He looked like one of those weird faces that Picasso painted, eyes and shit all over the place. My lobb-on had gone again. God how I laughed though. Scotchy and Cobalt were equally Picassofied, Cobalt doing his little Irish wrist-jig. Scotchy with his salivating face pressed hard up to the glass, nose all spread open, he looked like Lon Chaney's Phantom of the fucking Opera.

I would have to come back later on my own.

It was dark when we came out from the Tuggerama. The narrow streets were full of aggressive whores in brain damage make-up.

Tugging is thirsty work, so we headed on up to Cottage Cheese Faced Louie's. A real louche joint where you could get drunk till you started falling over and no-one gave a fuck. Old Louie he just carries on polishing his glasses, smiling benignly as a twelve-year-old girl sucks him off for drugs beneath the bar. Twelve being the age of consent in old donkey-shagging Spain, as all you Gary Glitter fans no doubt already know.

So I guess you can see how all this tipped us over the edge. Well me and Tex, Scotchy and Stargazer were too busy fiddling around with the digital inconsequels of our swansong album, *One More Knife*. Little known to my non-Black Magic chums, I decorated the inside cover with the most bum-out Tarot card in the whole deck, The Ten Of Swords. A picture of some poor

bastard nailed to the floor by ten massive battle swords. If that bit of black magic didn't finish us off for good, then nothing would.

I have no idea how long we were there for before some kind of blurred routine evolved.

We all shared a room in some radioactive hotel, Tuggy's Lounge we called it. It featured the usual broken landscape that reflected the dawn light's unwelcome gleaming. Beer and whiskey bottles all over the place, Empire State ash trays, porno mags with all the pages stuck together, unmade beds, unflushed toilets, furry takeaway food growing up the walls, filthy underwear, burnt peices of silver paper, coca cola tins with suspicious punctures – do I have to go on?

Tex and I would sluggishly wake around noon, finish off whatever booze was nearest before we even got out of bed, that's if we'd made it to bed, most of the time we'd wake with maybe one boot on, pants halfway down, lying where we fell.

In the bath, wrapped around the shitter, underneath the bed. One morning I found the Mexican arse cannon asleep face down, half inside the wardrobe, dried shit all down the back of his legs, a huge load filling up his dirty grey underpants. Flies buzzing around this prize faecal banquet.

It was a common mistake, I've often mistaken the wardrobe for the toilet in dozens of hotels.

We'd drink some breakfast down at the Cottage Cheese Face place, then up to the Tuggerama for some exercise, swigging more beers while our nads refuelled.

It was here in this degrading temple of wankdom that the first seeds of Tug Town were sown.

It was a mean town, just South of Tombstone and a couple of days' hard riding from Deadwood. A lot of guys died there, wanked themselves to death. It was those damn cabins. A fellah could disappear into one of those darn things and never get out. His skeleton found years later, a wad of tissue paper in his bony death hand, pants round his bony knees. A rancid tin of Bum OK snake oil overturned in the corner. TV screen almost opaque from well-aimed bollock oysters. "It would have been the way he wanted it."

"Yup, died with his cock in his hand, a proper tugger's death."

Now the sheriff of Tug Town he was a mean old bastard. The man weren't even a tugger, he'd taken the pledge after he saw his brother being taken out of The Tuggerama on a stretcher. Poor bastard died in the ambulance on the way to hospital. Chronic tuggism. He'd been holed up in one of those fucking cabins for over three months. From that day on the sheriff of Tug Town was determined to clean up this ungodly city of onanists and make it a place for decent folks to raise families and do fair trade.

The Tuggers hated him.

And that was it, we had invented Tug Town and it was going to be a hard climb to get out. We'd leave the Tuggerama, our eyes peeled for any sign of that bastard sheriff. The afternoons and early evenings were spent watching bullfights on those huge video screens in the bars around tugtown. The place had become so real now, we'd started getting jumpy. We'd heard rumours that the sheriff was fixing on driving us out of town. He'd placed marshalls outside the Tuggerama.

After watching a few hours of bulls being killed we headed on down to The Morrison hotel, which wasn't a hotel at all, but a small dimly lit bar with just the right essence of sleaze to make a man feel at home. The sheriff would never find us in here, it was the perfect hide-out.

Of course I fell in love with the chick who ran the place. Even after she tried to kill me. Actually if the truth be known it would probably have been more along the lines of assisting a suicide kind a thing; old Mary, she weren't exactly forcing that shit down my throat if you get my drift.

She was feeding me these huge vodkas and line after line of industrial strength cocaine right there on the bar. She couldn't speak English and Tex was so drunk he couldn't even speak Spanish any more, so all that word shit was effectively dealt with. Senora with the shining eyes and a bottom lip just the right size for the B side of my bell-end. Ting-a ling-a-ling, that's *amore*, sings Dino's pervoid cousin Pino.

I sat there at the bar just feasting my eyes on every single detail of her.

Her collarbones, prominent and long, the smooth angle of her back, as perfect as the neck of a swan. Long fingers and loose wrists, limbs and eyelashes like a giraffe. She moved like a giraffe as well, slowly with a rolling elegance.

If anyone out there is reading this and planning on becoming a public drunk, hardcore style – if you do insist on sitting at the bar dreaming your life away and falling in love with the girl who throws you your poison, then get up once in a while, check the wobble in your knees. There's nothing worse than

getting up off that barstool feeling like Hemingway or some other bogus tough guy and falling flat on your face like CoCo the fucking clown. Like I did, that night.

I fell on my face a few times on the way back to Tuggy's Lounge. It's not a good feeling. Blacking out, not remembering the actual fall, just the bang in your face as you hit concrete once again.

I was pretty fucked up the next day, so Tex boy went out solo. Fucking bastard had found himself a real chick. The fucker!

He'd bought himself a six pack of Budweiser to steel his nerve and make him feel like Clint Eastwood, and strolled in to Cottage Cheese Faced Louie's bar and hit on the chick that worked there. I was impressed, she was a looker. He said he knew she was dirty because he could see up her short sleeved shirt that she was wearing a blue bra.

Now that was even more impressive, the colour of a woman's lingerie as some indicator of sexual promiscuity.

He brings her back to Tuggy's Lounge and bones her right there amidst a pile of dirty underpants, even the flyblown banquet ones, you had to hand it to old Tex boy, he had class! I'm like reading *Danish Wankerwomen No 5* and old Texy boy's pimply arse is bucking into Spanish fly girl's slopping gash like something from a meat processing factory. Bitch seems to be enjoying herself but then starts moaning, she has a full bottle of whiskey in her hand and starts chugging on it as Mexican stud boy's ramming his shit-stained pimple butt up close to the vinegar stroke.

"Oh Tex, I am an alcoholic!!" she decides to tell him, shouting and slobbering in his ear. Beanboy bangs his bollock oyster into his rubber, flops off and throws the rubber onto the floor by the side of the mattress. I asked if he minded if I gave her one.

"Hey Zeddo, that's what friends are for," said the noble chap. I was glad he wore a johnny, I hate sloppy seconds, it's like gay or something. Cobalt didn't give a fuck, he was on next, stirring the gravy.

She was crying and stuff, swigging on her cheap whiskey, calling us rapists and all that other drunken shit. Tex locked her in the wardrobe, her crying was pissing us off. But you could still hear her muffled wailing. "For fuck's sake Tex," said Cobalt, flipping through *Sex Torture* magazine. "Either gaffa tape that cunt's mouth shut or throw her out of the fucking window, all that blubbing is pissing me off."

MARK MANNING

Old Texy pulls her out of the closet and asks if either of us wants to bugger her before he slings her out of the window. "No way man, alkies, their bungholes are always full of shit. Sling the cunt out and let's go check out some more bullfights," I said.

"Pass her over here man, she can suck me off before you get rid of her," said Cobalt.

The disgusting slut puked all over his sausage farm. Guitar boy goes berserk, calling her a disgusting human being and batters the shite out of her. Man that guy's got a fucking problem, hadn't he heard of all that women's lib shit, fucking Neanderthal. Tex thought better of throwing her out of the window and decided to give her an enema and then fuck her alkie arse before we went up to the bull fights.

We somehow managed to finish the album.

It was crap.

But we were great.

COUNTRY BOY LOVE

I really liked Johnny Boy. There was a naive innocence about the young sound engineer, that was altogether quite charming.

The thick cunt.

I don't remember where we found him, but I remember how we lost him, ears bleeding and completely gash-struck by some Munich slapper, a cheating wife that we all suspected had deflowered the innocent youngster. But more of that later.

It was a few days before we even spoke to him. If you're going on the road with someone, the intimacy that a tourbus affords means you have to get along.

Invisible walls are built, when someone is doing something in an idiosyncratic manner, no comment must be passed. Cobalt doing his fake press-ups and his weird karate. Me doing my cut-ups, snickering to myself, blind drunk at ten in the morning.

Suzy X and Tex Diablo's spam strangling. The pair of them, like Chinamen, slit eyes and front teeth biting their bottom lips, battering all unholy hell out of their poor beaten turkeys. No comment can be made at all, unless some stray bollock oyster splatters on the window from the stoned jizzologist sitting behind you.

You had to recognize that all of us need some form of private space. A little like being afloat on a small clipper, sleeping in tiny bunks, that were seriously defended. To even look in another guy's bunk was a serious hanging offence.

So after four or so days we decided the young chap with his Joe Orton drag was a fine fellow, and allowed him access to our fried and dangerous world.

He was so easy to wind up as well, not having that much battle experience.

I think it was probably his first time in Europe too. The look on his face as we browsed around the FUCK NOW tug shop had us in stitches, he was totally awed, never having seen hardcore shit before. His eyes lit up, a wanker's smile beaming beneath the carnal deluge of the FUCK NOW porno emporium. We all selected our publications and videos. But Johnny Boy was in some sort of trance, the avalanche of wanksterbation had him under some sort of spell. He ran around the place and bought a few items in brown paper bags, running back to the tour bus to play with himself.

MARK MANNING

Ordinarily one doesn't comment about another man's tug of choice, but Johnny was so cute we couldn't resist.

It was Phil Shit, the tour manager who started it. Picked up Johnny's copy of *Backside Girls*, giving Johnny a theatrically incomprehensible look. Grimacing as if he'd just seen a trio of arse queens all tangled all up in a sailor's knot of buggering and bell-endery. *Backside Girls* was a small colour magazine with numerous studies of women bending over and pulling their arse cheeks apart, the arsehole being the main focus of the picture. A few of them smiled over their shoulders, but it was obviously the ringpiece that was what the picture was all about. To be quite honest it looked as if a few of those Euro trollops didn't even wipe their arses properly. "There's something facking wrong with you mate," said the coach driver. That was it, we all piled in, laughing at what stoked his monkey. "You never see birds' arseholes in English magazines," protested the shame-faced tugger. "Fucking right you don't," said Robbie. "Who fucking wants to!" Even though the hypocritical bumhole through the knickers man was quite fond of sucking on a bird's tin can himself.

We couldn't stop laughing for the whole tour, he had another name now.

Johnny Starfish. God, the poor little bastard, he must have rued the day he came across those backside babes.

You only had to look at him with his little Joe Orton cap and say his name and you risked breaking a rib through laughing.

Backside girls. I'm laughing myself stupid even as I tell this tale.

He was an excellent sport though, and took all the piss-ripping like a decent tugger.

Apart from his love of women's bumholes, Johnny had another passion. He was a huge fan of the work of Joe Meek, the sixties British producer who developed a sound that challenged Phil Spector for its strange, Telstar uniqueness.

Johnny Starfish had tapes of all the man's songs. Naïve John Boy had no idea that Meek was a backside man himself, only it was backside *boys* old Joey was interested in.

A lot of Meek's work was so camp you couldn't stop laughing. Johnny didn't know why we were laughing, the unworldly son of Bristol. Meek's work was recorded in the sixties, most people then didn't believe that homosexuals really existed, which gave our fruity brothers great leeway for their double

entendres and saucy jokes. *Round The Horne*, Julian and Sandy. Even well into the seventies, Larry Grayson shutting his door with slack Alice, these fuckers got away with murder, entertaining grannies on prime time TV with all manner of hilarious buggery jokes.

So of course Joe Meek and his cutesy protégé Heinz, a peroxide blonde, banged out some of the campest records ever made. One in particular had us choking on our beer, eyes wet with tears of laughter. It was called "Country Boy Love", I wish I could remember more of the lyrics but us ladies were too busy laughing to even hear it properly. Something like "Country boy love is as good as any other". You could almost see the finger on his eyebrow and left hand on his hip as cheeky little Heinz baby minced across the vinyl.

It spawned another tour game that we never got bored of, trundling backwards and forwards binned out of our heads across the Alps. "Country Boy Love" miming.

We all took it in turns to mime to the bumboy classic. I think Robbie got the first prize, it was his ringpiece-flashing that did the trick. But fucking Tex man, that Mexican bastard looked like some evil tarantula luring small children into his cave, it still scares me now just thinking about it. In his black cowboy hat, bottle of Mescal in his hand, tortoiseshell cigarette holder, long black leather limbs. Almost as bad as when Slam and myself, fried and drunk, genuinely believed that Cobalt was one of the undead, a fucking vampire. I shit you not fellow heads.

He never surfaced from his bunk/coffin during daylight hours, only surfacing after nightfall. But our real suspicions were almost tragically sent careering into madness when we found out that he slept in his sunglasses. He didn't like garlic sausage either. This in a man whose favourite food is raw peas out of their pods, and tripe and onions. Slam, who wasn't joking, put a silver crucifix above his own bunk and a couple of cloves of garlic and a stolen Gideons bible under his pillow. He started following Cobalt around for nights noting that the suspect vampire avoided all mirrors.

We checked Dracula's bunk for clues when he was in the shitter. A massive bog roll and pornography that we couldn't understand. Pictures of naked women in car crashes. Japanese girls with their limbs in plaster casts and bandages. A copy of a very well-thumbed *Grays Anatomy* with the pages stuck together.

Slam was freaked, convinced that the guitarist was the Prince of Darkness.

MARK MANNING

Wanted to do him during the day with a stake. I reasoned with the poor confused drummer telling him that if Cobalt really was one of the undead that we should at least wait till the tour was over before we beheaded the evil one. We still had loads of gigs to do. I eventually convinced him that maybe it was all that skunk and other shit we'd been poaching our brains with for God knows how long.

It seemed to work, but Transylvanian Tommy still gave us the creeps, sat there in the darkness playing *Mortal Kombat* in his shades. Face illuminated like some kind of Bela Lugosi in Raybans and a NY baseball cap.

But back to old John the starfish, and the popping of his long overdue cherry. And the terrible consequences.

We'd never seen anything like it.

The gash-crossed lover. You couldn't invent this stuff. It almost made up for nearly killing ourselves with rock and no money. That poor little sod.

Victim of the gash.

Apart from the standard road gash, which was basically anything that didn't make you want to throw up, there were a couple of other categories. Standby gash, which was any female from the record company who had been assigned to look after us for difficult things like remembering our own names and checking into hotels. They were OK in an emergency but the downside to them was that they didn't disappear, like road gash did. It was usually OK though because they tended to feel so disgusted with themselves the next morning, they found one reason or another to disapppear anyway.

When there was no standby gash there was usually some subnormal bottom of the barrel gash hanging around, Gimpo for reasons known only to himself used to let them travel on the bus with us. We didn't mind as long as he gave them strict orders not to look at us. They had to travel at the front as well, with the sweaty-arsed crew.

She was a mean one, this one. She was part of that gaggle of hornsmokers that we had named The Wild Wives of Munich.

They'd telephoned husbands and boyfriends with ludicrous lies about how they were away on some business shit and hopped onto our Leviathan of depravity, the ghastly six-wheeled tourbus. Das Bus we called it. A foul thing that smelled like a barnyard.

Obviously I have no recollection of that first evening sliding further and further into sexual hell, but the next morning, there's old Johnny boy, arm

around his cheating slutbitch, Munich shagbag, smoking langorously, pleased as fuck with himself, smiling like the kingliest king of sex in the world. It was obvious that this was the first fuck of his life.

Sperm girl wandered off to powder her cunt, or whatever they do in that small room.

"So you fucked her then John boy," said Robbie, barely avoiding bursting into hysterics. "Of course," said studboy, with a self-satisfied smile and a smug wobble of the head that would have shamed James fucking Bond.

Oh man, we were creased up, almost sick with laughter for nearly four days. When we found out that Johnny had asked her to marry him, well we just shit our pants and called for a doctor for something to stop us laughing ourselves to death.

Talk about gash-struck, the fucking idiot makes up some ridiculous story about his ears bleeding and mooned off the tour. High-tailing it down to Munich with super trollope and his aching blütwurst. Things didn't quite work out with his romantic dream of settling down and having sex all day with his mädchen though.

It seems like Fraülein Hornsmoker had a very jealous husband who had discovered all about the gash-crossed lovers and in no uncertain terms, armed with his hunting rifle, had told young John boy to get out of town. Krauts with guns. Woah!

Johnny for once, made the right decision and caught the first plane home. A tear in his eye and a broken spunkbone.

TO THE MANOR BORED

"There's something fucking wrong with these trout," said Cobalt, pulling out his fifteenth fat rainbow in as many minutes. "They're not supposed to just jump on your maggot as soon as you throw your hook in," he explained, the keen angler, all perplexed.

"They're rock star trout," I replied. "Branson has them specially trained, imagine if Elton or Freddy went fishing and they didn't catch a fish within five minutes, they'd throw a tantrum and pull the session."

We were at The Manor, Richard Branson's ridiculously opulent recording studio in Oxfordshire. We fucking hated it. Sent us all mad.

"Where's Kid Chaos?" said Cobalt torturing one of his fish, poking its eyes out with a disgorger.

"Down in the swimming pool with his remote control U-boat," I replied, appalled at Cobalt's fish cruelty.

"Slammy?"

"Composing music on his drums."

This was back in the eighties. There was some kind of economic shit going down. Reaganomics, Mrs Thatcher was in on it somewhere. I'm not sure of the exact details but from what I could gather it all seemed to be about borrowing shit loads of money and not paying it back.

I could deal with that.

Cosmosodomistic Records had advanced us in some form or another just over a million quid, if they thought there was any way they were going to get that sort of money back on their Reagamaniacal investment then they deserved to be fleeced.

We'd just signed some ridiculous deal and before the sperm was even dry on the first groupie's face, the cosmosodomistic motherfuckers had set about trying to destroy the band.

Charlie Bumfucker our public school-educated AR man, had sounded the death knell the minute he produced a copy of *Slippery When Wet*, the multi-billion selling album by Cosmosodomistic golden wonderboys Bon Jovi, and said he wanted us to sound like them.

How anyone in their right mind, anyone with the merest hint of a brain cell could possibly imagine that we could ever, even if we wanted to, sound like the polished turdosity that was Bon Jovi defies human comprehension.

We were a dirty, sleazy, obscene, sexual gutter monster of a thing. We had all taken far too many drugs, were all borderline psychotics and all of us alcoholics to the man.

We weren't career-conscious rock social climbers, we didn't want awards, number ones and all the other shit that record companies covet.

We wanted to rock.

I knew the whole thing wasn't going to work on the day we signed the deal. The MD, I can't even remember his name, some dealer with too much money and an ugly wife talked down to us.

Deep sin.

I mean sure, most musicians are pretty simple, that's why we're so good at what we do. Our entire being is focused in an almost autistic fashion into producing something so transient, ethereal and beautiful that it consumes every other part of our psychological development. This savant-like state of being is utterly and completely incomprehensible to people of an executive nature.

They just think that we're stupid.

We think that they're evil.

Both assumptions, of course, being way off the mark.

I handed the signing pen to Hymie Uglywife and caught a look in his eye that told me he knew all this as well as me.

I had a decision to make.

Was I going to bang my head against a brick wall of heartache and frustration for the next two years, or was I going to enjoy the ride.

I fastened my seatbelt.

The record industry is a strange beast.

A fat sprawling monster that spunks dollars, has a million heads and no brain.

Of course the mavericks and geniuses that occasionally ride this beast are instinctively aware of this and do not attempt to instil any order or discipline upon their wild golden geese.

Unfortunately, mavericks and geniuses are rare creatures and for every genuine midwife of sublime creativity there are a thousand dunderheads.

We were plagued by dunderheads.

"What I want you to do is like, create an enviroment. Candles, flags,

Everything is holy –
even the nuclear bomb

ZODIAC MINDWARP

crystals, all the shit that you like, make this place your own," said Steve, the producer.

The last record he'd produced was The Cult's *Love* album. It worked for them.

All that quasi-magical shit, creating an atmosphere of unreality that enabled them to access their creative genius.

We didn't need the theatrics. We were totally at ease with our divine madness. We were mad for fuck's sake.

Steve farted. "Oh shit, I think I've followed through," said Range Rover boy rushing off to the toilet to wash his arse.

"Who is that fucking guy?" said Slam, fanning the air in front of his nose.

"Some producer cat," I said. "Cosmosodomistic sorted him out, he's like, producing us or something."

"What *is* production?" asked Cobalt, sagely.

"I think it's like a guy that like, sits around behind the spaceship controls and says do it again, or something, when you already know that you've played a bum note or something, kind of," I said, ripping off a ring pull and decking half a can of Tennants super.

"Yeah, right, but what's he doing here?" offered Slam, playing with a Barbie doll, pulling down her pants and seeing if she had a cunt. She didn't, they never do, but for some reason you just can't help checking every one you come across.

"Well basically, he gets payed shit loads of money and has to kind of kiss our arses and also kiss the record company arses and then he gets like loads more money," I said, not really understanding what I was saying, but knowing I was right.

"Yeah, but he's got a Range Rover," said Kid Chaos, who was the youngest of our crew and still stupid enough to be impressed by those kind of things.

"Yeah well, we're here, and he is, we've got like free food and like, loads of fucking amps. Let's just rock." Cobalt Stargazer. Pure, unadulterated genius.

This shit went on for days.

Nobody really knowing what we were doing.

Steve was a record producer and he had diarrhoea.

His attempts to bond with us were truly pathetic.

His experience with rock bands had led him to believe that rock bands were all complete idiots and that the flimsiest forms of psychological manipulation

would suffice in getting us to record "Slimy When Slack".

I mean it was cool, don't get me wrong.

Free money is always a blast.

It's not everyday that you get some gay gourmet chef cooking up fancy food for you that you don't even like.

"Can we go from the top again boys," said Steve the shite arse.

"Yeah man, we can go from the side as well if you want," I replied. There was no way this cunt was going to get a piece of us.

I believed and I still do, that the recorded evidence of what as a band The Love Reaction do is sublime and holy.

Mr Brownarse brought commerce into our church. And quite frankly we were having none of it.

All down the line we sabotaged any of his attempts to wring prayers from us. We were an elite order. This motherfucker Steve Diarrhoea-arse was an agent of Satan. A keeper of the black gas hornets hiving poison eggs in the arse-crack of our minds. An employee of Cosmosodomistic Records Inc. – and as such he could fuck right off.

Now Bill Drummond is a man who I have total respect for.

He is not perfect, which probably goes a long way in explaining why I love him so much.

Bill knows he is not perfect. Would be the first person to tell you about what a complete fucking arsehole he is.

But he would tell you with eloquence, and with style.

The thing about Bill is, he knows what rock and roll is.

In his bones, in his soul, he understands.

If anyone was to produce the Love Reaction, it had to be Bill.

Unfortunately he brought his friend, his friend and our manager, Dave Fucking Balfe with him.

For every inspired notion Bill came up with, for every mentaloid riff Cobalt slung, the Balfe would be there with his stopwatch and slide rule, banging it down and talking about algebra.

Tattooed Beat Messiah was nearly the eighth greatest record ever made.

But Balfe made sure it wasn't.

His pedantry and negative charm scuppered the whole show.

And that's the way it was meant to be.

MARK MANNING

Balfe, God bless him, he gave us tomorrow.
WE STILL HAD TO – and still *have* to – MAKE A HALFWAY DECENT
RECORD.

When I was writing this book, after about nine months of concerted rambling I took in what I thought was the completed manuscript for James and Miranda to peruse and mumble over.

"How many words is that, do you reckon, Miranda?" said the black-clad editor.

"Hmm, no more than about forty thousand," replied his assistant, Nazi torturer and evil killer of men, Miranda Wordcount.

"Hmm yeah, thought so, we'll probably need about the same amount again Z," said James apologetically. "You've got two weeks."

"We could maybe double space it..." said Miranda, seeing the look of sheer panic blanche across my face.

"Nah, you can do it, can't you Z, just chain yourself to your computer man," said James, who assumes that everyone is as prolific a genius as he and his eight million literary alter egoes.

"Erm yeah, no problem, I'll just go off and get started now," I replied, panicking like a fucker and bumbling into the nearest off license to search for inspiration.

"Yeah Z, it's James," said the phone the next day. "Do you fancy a beer man, I've made some notes." I pulled on my pants and walked the twenty or so yards across the road to my publisher's local. James never goes further than the corner of his street – to the Clockhouse pub in Clerkenwell – unless it's on a trip to Japan. An admirable state of affairs, I think everyone would agree.

I mention all of this as one of the subjects James suggested I should write about in his notes was the writing of song lyrics.

This struck me as somewhat unique, since in all the ten gazillion times I've been interviewed by rock journos around the world, not one of them ever asked me about the lyrics to any of our songs.

So how *do* you write a song lyric?

I'm tempted to say that it's a piece of piss and that anyone can do it, for my own sake more than anything else. I try to believe that this writing shit is easy and nothing special. This is mainly to try and ameliorate the terrible, dreadful feeling that one day my muse, like some stabled wild horse, will bolt, leap over the stable doors and gallop off into the hills never to be seen

ZɐDIⱯC

again. Will vanish, melt like snow.

That in the middle of the night I will be visited by that secret, unholy terror, Writer's Block. The sheer inconceivable, mind-shivering, spleen-rupturing dread that one day you might wake up in your head and be alone.

And muse baby, she's gone.

Your number one fan.

That wonderful, wonderful girl that thinks that everything you do is fantastic.

Actually, even mentioning her existence is spooking the fragile thing and scaring the living shite out of me, so if it's all the same to you, dear reader, I'll keep this one short and move on.

Muses.

They're very touchy.

Don't like being talked about.

BIBLE OF DREAMS

Of course I nicked the title from Sylvia Plath and her grumpy little book; *Johnny Panic And The Bible of Dreams*.

And that's the only comparison.

The title, that is.

My *Bible Of Dreams* is a truly mad book and it still scares the shit out of me even now, whenever I dare look at it.

It's a weird collection of scary collage and deranged juxtaposition with all manner of schizophrenic prophesy and narrative dripping from its guts.

I stitched and glued it together in the snowy wastes of the arctic in 1994.

Sometimes I wished I hadn't.

Bill Drummond the brilliant essayist, artist and world famous trumper described it as a visual poem, even financing and writing a commentary for a ridiculously luxurious and opulent reproduction of the original. Which, incidentally, is currently being guarded by the actor, Satanist and libertine Keith "Billy Shagnasty" Allen.

Keith is the only man alive who is evil enough to withstand the book's supernatural powers.

The reason it scares me so much is that it reminds me of just how far out you can get on long North European tours.

The evidence contained in that monster grimoire makes it pretty clear that it's a far far long fucking way, and sometimes some people don't ever quite make it all the way back.

Slam Thunderhide, our drummer poet was standing by some fjörd way up in the Arctic Circle, he looked pensive and ill at ease, talking to himself, as the sensitive sticksman often did.

It was early evening, a faint flicker of the Aurora Borealis shimmered above the distant mountains on the other side of the still water.

Slam was sharing a hotel room with the Stargazer, as he always did.

Sometimes the Stargazer's rampant, jizz-raging boneology, buggering, shagging, raping and torturing anything with a heartbeat and a pair of tits got to him.

As I said, he was a sensitive lad, he wrote love poetry and liked to wear women's clothes to relax in sometimes.

MARK MANNING

Not that there was anything homosexual about him or anything, he just liked the sensual feeling of women's silk underwear and the restrictive nature of corsetry next to his sensitive poet boy skin.

He said that it enabled him more easily to get in touch with the feminine side of his nature. This is not as uncommon as you would imagine, for example Motorhead's Lemmy is well known in rock circles as an avid cross-dresser, being particularly fond of donning antique women's land army cami-knickers.

I wandered over to my perplexed-looking friend and put a concerned arm around his shoulder. I knew he was feeling stressed out as I could feel his bra strap beneath his "Fuck Off" T-shirt.

As a band we looked out for each other, buoying each other's spirits up when they started to flag. Existential despair, suicidal gloom, venereal depression, that sort of shit. Slammy was particularly prone to the suicidal shit. We were continually finding long rambling suicide notes written in the Canadian's distinctive spiky scrawl all over the place. Slam would get drunk on cheap vodka, write out his last words then fall asleep before getting round to jumping out of the bus or whatever novel method of shuffling off his mortal coil he'd thought of that week.

"You OK Slam?" I said breezily, offering him a hit on my hip flask. Usually a good drink and a few jokes lifted Johnny Suicide's mood; I knew all of my band members well, as they did me.

"Yeah man," he answered, but I knew he wasn't. "It's just Cobalt, he's up in the hotel room, him and Gimpo are farting around with some tramp, I don't know, sometimes..." He tailed off.

A lot of the time I got the feeling that Slam didn't really have the stomach for the horrendous levels of madness and debauchery that touring inevitably choked up in its wake. "God you know Z," he continued urgently, "I used to be like a normal fucking guy, had a fucking life, had a fucking wife, everything man.... And now like I'm here in this fucking... this fucking... I don't even fucking know where I am, is this still fucking Germany? What's all this snow shit man?" ejaculated the confused drummer.

Touring often gets that way, you lose interest in destinations and locality, countries and cities blur into each other creating a sometimes distressing sense of dislocation. "I've got VD and there's some bitch tied up in my bath tub!" Slam was almost in tears. "Cobalt's shitting on her tits. I wouldn't mind

man but it fucking stinks, you know what I'm saying, she's a fucking pig as well man," he added, shaking his head in disbelief. I didn't know whether he was shocked by the turdology or the fact that the young woman was particularly unattractive.

"Cobalt's shitting on her?" I said, surprised. I knew Gimpo liked to crap on women but I didn't realise Cobalt had started to sink into that end of the game. He was always a bondage and mild torture man, I guess this tour must have been getting to us in more ways than was usual. Ordinarily the really gruesome stuff doesn't start till at least two months into a prolonged excursion.

Slam sucked on the whiskey and laughed. "You know what I mean Z, I mean this crap's like just getting fucking normal to me man. I mean how fucking long is it going to be till I start shitting in women's fucking faces and stuff. You know, like I get home to the wife, Hi honey I'm home and then like throw her on the floor and start unloading the boulders and soup all over her fucking chops. Jesus... I mean those fucking eels in Dresden man, you know what I'm saying..."

Slam's mood had lifted slightly as he tried to understand the totally surreal world of a hard-working rocker. "Like I get home or something and say like, the Mrs has some of her normal friends around, dinner party bullshit, chit chat, oh yes at the office today, Julia blah blah I mean what do I say? What are my witty little anecdotes going to fucking sound like to Julia and fucking Charles? Oh yeah we all buggered this girl, it was so funny, you had to have been there, Gimpo stuffed a tortoise up her arse and we all shat in her handbag, fucking hell man, you know what I'm fucking saying?"

I knew exactly what he was saying. I had my own way of dealing with this dilemma though, when I wasn't on tour I simply wouldn't see anyone at all. Lock myself away with a crate of vodka, a huge stash of buggery videos and wait patiently for the next tour.

The tortoise up the arse was a reference to the bag of live eels the Gimp had bought the previous week.

That poor girl.

Gimpo had gaffa taped the little fourteen-year-old face down onto the dressing room table and was laughing like a demon. Her cheeky little arse wriggled frantically as he took his slippery two foot pets from their sack. I dont think I'll ever forget the look of absolute shock and brain-dribbling

MARK MANNING

terror that flashed across her face when she realised what was about to happen to her. I'm just glad he had the good sense to gag her before he started bunging them up her.

I felt a bit bad about the eel incident though, as I knew that Gimpo had got the idea from my bible.

"Man I knew this was going to be a weird tour when I saw you getting on the bus with that huge silver fucking book," said Slam laughing, the whiskey seemed to have lightened him up. "Fuck it, I'm just being stupid, let's go shit on that cunt in Cobalt's bath or something." He laughed again and ran off to the hotel to get into a bit of light-hearted coprophilia.

Long tours can be fucking boring.

Sure the show and the attendant squalor and mind-blowing depravity with the local spunkbuckets afterwards is always amusing. Especially if Gimpo has got a bag of eels and some fireworks, but it's the bit before the gig that can grind you down.

You arrive in some strange town early in the morning after travelling all night on your rolling barnyard and there's nothing to do until two in the afternoon, when the venue opens to allow you to soundcheck.

That was the main reason I'd brought along my silver A3 sketch pad. I wasn't sure what I was going to fill it with, maybe drawings or something, I just needed something to while away those dead hours with, otherwise I'd just end up getting drunk all the time. Unfortunately, being an alcoholic, if I don't have anything to occupy me I tend to just get completely shit-faced and, to be quite honest, it was starting to worry me a little around this time.

The drink had already cost me two marriages and I didn't want to blow the third one (of course I did, but I didn't know that was going to happen at the time).

Unlike Cobalt and the rest of the band who just stay on the bus masturbating and farting, in most cities we would visit I would always make an effort to visit the local church or cathedral.

And the porn shop.

I have invented a strange religion for myself that finds the two places not entirely incompatible amidst my highly idiosyncratic catechism.

Madonna and child, the sanctity of motherhood.

I can't be arsed explaining it all here but I'm sure you get the gist, something

along the line about how shagging is holy, that kind of auto-didactic bollocks. Well it works for me anyway.

My bible of dreams was some kind of attempt to illustrate my odd heresy without using words.

On that tour bus, amongst the frozen wastes and icy fjörd, strange theories and assumptions could – and did – take root. I had decided I was going to create a holy book. My reasoning had been circling for some time around the notion that literal interpretations of all religions were the cause of all the sufferings of the world.

So therefore if my holy book did not contain any words, there could be no literal interpretation, hence no suffering.

I told you man, shit gets weird out there in the snow.

I was on a mission, yet again.

It's part of my thing, I know you can get pills for it, but shit, life is so boring when you don't go crazy and have a mission now and again.

I still hold to that, as any intelligent person would.

The art commisioned by religion's canon contains most if not all of the most beautiful, sublime and holy things ever created by man.

I mean I wasn't aiming for a Cistine chapel kind of thing, but I reckoned I could match some old illuminating friar.

My holy book was to be entirely visual.

Like that other scripture of esoteric wisdom, the Tarot.

It would contain parables, prophesy, truth and wisdom.

It would also have evidence of the hand of the Devil.

All holy books contain evidence of Old Scratch's wicked humour.

I set about collecting things that I liked. Scraps of paper found in the street, restaurant menus, matchboxes with interesting images on them. I went for all the usual symbolic shit, things with images of lighthouses, lifeboats, fires, stars, angels, and stuff on them. I also collected odder things like fly-fishing floats and children's comics.

I raided the cathedrals for bibles in Scandinavian languages.

And shit loads of porn.

Shit loads of porn.

I don't know exactly what it is about pornography, I mean it had gone way beyond just the wanking stage for me at the time. I mean my own personal taste just involved the usual vanilla shit, blow jobs, shagging and a bit of bondage and buggery.

Maybe the odd dog-shagging stuff, but some of the shit you could get in these cathedrals of tuggism, they defied human comprehension.

Hence the eel incident.

And somehow all of this, this variety of sexuality, this sheer weirdness and perverse joy, there was something holy in all of that as well.

I mean really, who gives a shit if you want to dress up as Frankenstein and shove rubber sharks up your wife's arse, if you get my drift.

Milking mamas, I mean to be quite honest, lactating, good God, please no.

Sour tit milk, have you ever whiffed that?

On the bed sheets, the following morning, when mama's too tired to clean it up.

I don't know. I mean all of that Milky Mama shit got tangled up in there with the Madonna and child.

Dog-shagging and Leda and the Swan, the legends of ancient Greece, Europa and all that other animal-shagging stuff.

There is a theory that schizophrenia is like some mad TV remote control that just zaps through every piece of information that's coming in and makes random connections.

Maybe that's all that my bible of dreams really was.

A schizo's diary.

That assumpton has been made, by none other than Ian Sinclair, and let's face it, old ancient connections loony boy, if anyone should fucking know it's him.

But I personally don't think it is the work of a schizophrenic.

Mainly because I'm not schizophrenic, are we Z.

I just make unusual connections. "The only difference between myself and a madman is that I'm not mad," said that great masturbator Salvador Dali, which I offer as my defence against anyone questioning my motivations and output.

It's a cute paradox and an amusing axiom much appreciated by all serious students of Zen buddhism, that the more knowledge a person acquires the more crazy he appears.

Dotty professors and eccentric scientists bumble their way across our modern cinematic mythopoeia like dishevelled starlings without any undue comment, India teems with holy fools, Saddhus blasted on spliff, bollock

naked, laughing at the universe. Maybe my voracious appetite for knowledge of everything, from the sparkling electric poetry of quantum physics to the musky pages of books detailing the anal techniques of seventeenth century homosexual pirates, was all just confusing me.

Perhaps the connections I was making between St Sebastiane and the SM bumfoolery of Germany's butchest bumboys, *Milky Mamas* and the birth of the milky way, *Animal Farm* and the zoophilia of the greeks, Jesus Christ and Walt Disney's Dumbo the elephant were all pushing it a bit too far.

Maybe the world would never be ready for pictorial allegories linking The Virgin Mary, motherhood, Jesus crucified and spunking cocks.

Maybe I really am just a nut.

Or maybe, like Bill says in the bible's introduction, it really is one of the holiest books ever made.

Five hundred quid John.

Send me the cash care of Creation Books, and you can either make up or lose your own mind.

ONE MONKEY, ONE STICK OF DYNAMITE AND A BOX OF MATCHES

As a band we generally had a pretty positive outlook on life.

Positive to the point of rank criminality if the truth were known.

I mean if we met someone and they told us that they were a murderer our response would be somewhere along the lines of "well I'm sure you had your reasons".

If the paedophile child rapist wanker bastard told us that he had wandered into a school and killed fifteen kids with his bare penis we would probably just assume that the guy was having a bad hair day.

One of the kids was ours?

Well I guess I needn't bother picking her up from school later then.

That's the breezy, cheerful kind of guys that we were.

I explain this in order that you can understand why we decided to give Gimpo the job as our manager. And why still to this day he has not forgiven us for, you guessed it, sacking him.

"You fucking sacked me!" invariably goes the shout somewhere halfway down the road to the alcohol/cocaine misery that is known as having a good time.

Let me explain.

As a rocking outfit, The Love Reaction had not come up to David Balfe's mendacious expectations.

We were too intelligent.

Now, in most walks of life, intelligence is mainly seen as an asset (apart from the armed forces, police and government that is, but we won't go into that one here).

To gain success, shameful amounts of money and obscene drug and mental health problems in that grail of rock manager heaven, America, you have to be totally compliant, stupid and have an accomodating arsehole.

That's just the way it works.

You roll over and get fucked.

By every Arnie toilet cleaner fucking Fufkin and every Sir Hymie Bottleswank cosmosodomistic record company screaming big baby MD on the entire continent.

The thing about America, the place where all the money comes from, is that they are not very bright. I mean I know this has been said eight billion times before, but fuck it, it's true. Maybe it's got something to do with the sprightly nature of the country's youth. I mean it's only yesterday that they reluctantly set all their slaves free – after the work was done – and all the native Indians were pretty much genocided by stealth out of existence. They haven't had that extra two thousand or so years to build up a healthy disrespect and cynicism towards their elected rulers.

But whatever it is, in America the game has to be played straight.

You are a can of beans and as such you are sold while your flavour is hot.

No complications like thinking you are an artist, trying to subvert the values of Western culture, deluded notions of trying to speed the evolution of your species or any of that other drug-addled nonsense.

You sing pretty songs about loving girls and being lonely occasionally and are rewarded with enough money to make you unhappy for the rest of your life.

We just didn't get that.

We were on a mission.

Like all over-indulged spoilt brats we wanted, like our idol Adolf Hitler, to destroy the world.

So, thank God, we got Gimpo to manage us.

He did an excellent job.

In the space of just under one year we went from playing New York humongodromes to playing support at The Arse and Racket pub in Camden Town.

Now Gimpo, being as intelligent as he was, decided in his position as big executive manager boy, with like a suit and a shiny pair of brogues, to employ himself a fetching little assistant.

Emma Tulip, nineteen years old, with the cutest, buggerable little arse that ever wiggled down from the provinces.

Now little Emma was no mug, she knew exactly what Gimpo wanted.

And what he wanted, she made damn sure that he didn't get. Her cute buggerable little arse that is. The rest of the band got to have a ride on it but poor old Gimps had to keep on pummelling in five-knuckle frenzy.

Little arse-shagging Miss Tulip was great, all the guys with free money for bands loved her.

We sacked the Gimp and got buggery girl Tulip to be our prostitute.

MARK MANNING

We were convinced that with her cocksucking skills and her pert bumhole she would be able to shag us a deal in no time.

Wrong.

The thing is, old tulip lips wasn't that clever a whore and set her sights far too low.

For her, cocaine and fancy hotels, champagne and the odd flash restaurant were all that were required to access her prime asset.

Strictly amateur hour.

Those middle-aged sleazebags with pony tails saw her coming a mile off. She gave it her best though, sucked off half of the arseholes that sleaze up the corridors of Radio One. Let the managers of several of the world's biggest acts bum her blind in hotels all over London. But once they had had their way, like most rich and powerful men, they tripped along to the next teenage virgin bumhole wafting in from the sticks.

Poor Emma, I almost felt sorry for her.

After realising that there was no-one on Earth that would have anything to do with a bunch of arse terrorist, Nazi, alcoholic drug-fiend space-rapists like the Love Reaction she packed up her prolapsed rectum, forged a band cheque for two thousand quid and whimpered back to where she came from. Her long-suffering teenage sweetheart of course took her back, ruptured bumhole and everything.

Toilets in the West End, cocaine, hotels, restaurants, night clubs, managers of big international rock bands, teenage bumholes, Gimpo, the original monkey with the dynamite, you know the score.

Boom, baby, fucking boom.

"You sacked me!"

AND FUCKING CASHEW NUTS AS WELL

Our manager David Balfe, the cunning, scheming usurer, realised that there was no way he was ever going to be able bribe us to make anywhere near the penis-dribbling, synapse-melting billions of dollars that he dearly coveted in his life. Even more so than underage chutney.

All of his cheating, sexually depraved, wife and child abusing career he had dreamed of that elusive chimera. American chart success.

With his ex-boyfriend and fellow analologist, hippy bummer Julius Dope they had tried for years with their gayish rock band My Arsehole's Just Exploded to reap the brown pound, but with no luck. Gay rock was massive in the early eighties when the Arseholes were big, but American success had always eluded him.

But not this time.

The Love Reaction would do the business. Or so he thought.

OK they didn't play gay rock but they were all good looking and it sounded sort of like heavy metal which is all gay anyway isn't it?

How could it fail?

In his mean cave of masturbation and avarice he devised a sneaky plan that he hoped would bring him treasure and gold beyond his wildest dreams. Enough money to buy as many little orphan buggery children from the internet as he wanted.

We were convinced that Balfe, apart from money, liked nothing more than buggering little orphan buggery children to death. And eating them.

Dave's plan was simple.

He would sell a percentage of his magic goose, Zodiac Mindwarp and The Love Reaction. Something of something being better than nothing of nothing, the shrewd Jew reasoned to himself as he started masturbating, thinking about toilets and money.

Of course he was still unaware at the time that myself and the Love Reaction were just pretty much ordinary geese and if any of us were concealing any golden eggs up our arses well, we were keeping damn quiet about them.

The slimy, Fagin-like Balfe stroked his greasy beard and sucked a piece of human baby meat from between his teeth. He farted loudly and turned the pages of his industrial pornography magazine before wanking himself off yet again and quickly jizzing off onto a picture of a mongol being buggered by a

fat German man dressed up as Frankenstein.

He threw the magazine into his porno trunk along with all his other hideously depraved publications and wiped his bell-end onto the blazer of a schoolboy he had murdered earlier that week.

The evil Jew reached for another even more sinister magazine.

He smiled and rubbed the shiny cover.

"The top twenty U.S. managers who are easily manipulated by snidy British arsehole bastard wanker managers today," he read aloud, and started giggling.

It was a very strange and rare publication indeed.

A business periodical.

Balfe thumbed through the magazine, looking at the pictures. Gruesome photographs of fat men with cigars having sex with very young children and obviously deeply distressed animals. A look of salacious satisfaction drooling across their hideously inbred faces.

Balfe's plan was to go into partnership with an established management company in the United States who, using their knowledge and influence in the market, could hopefully bring in the obscene amounts of money Balfe needed to sate his squalid desires.

With the aid of his lawyer, Israel Belsen he was planning on sneaking in some technicality into the legal agreement that would ensure that everyone would be shafted apart from himself.

Belsen was a canny music businesss lawyer and had an outstanding reputation for stiffing hundreds of innocent musicians and their young families and serious drug habits.

The pair worked long into the night, cackling in the candlelit offices of the Belsen, Belsen and Dachau law partnership like a pair of hideous demons lurking in the vile satanic canon of the Hebrew religion.

Belsen, Belsen and Dachau were Kabbalistic music lawyers who had formed their conspiratorial partnership in the late sixties and had only one aim in life: to be completeley evil and to ruin everything for everyone.

Balfe loved them.

Rod Smallwood and his business partner Elie Taylor were quite unique in the world of rock management. Neither one of the multi-millionaire impressarios were paedophiles and although Elie was of Jewish ancestry he

assured me that he had never felt the slightest inclination towards ritually murdering a gentile child in his entire life...

Both upstanding citizens enjoyed nothing more than doing charity work with handicapped youngsters, often inviting the severely disabled little chaps back to their luxury Beverly Hills mansions for sleepovers.

Their kindness to the underprivileged and their unceasing philanthropic concern for those less fortunate than themselves made them appear in Dave Balfe's eyes to be a right couple of fucking mugs.

Balfe's cynicism dictated that anyone who did good work and cared about other people apart from themselves must be a complete idiot, and therefore a piece of piss to cheat.

The evil British manager and his equally heinous lawyer Israel Belsen fine-tuned the small print on their odious contract, laughed demonically and toasted each other's genius with murdered child blood.

As usual Cobalt ordered the most expensive thing on the menu and, so as not to be outdone, I ordered two of the same thing.

Rod and Elie had deep pockets. It was our first meeting with these fabulously wealthy entrepreneurial philanthropists and they had taken us to the most expensive restaurant in London, Le Cunt in London's exclusive Mayfair.

On the table next to us The Princess of Wales, before her tragic death – that incidentally, really made me cry – was flirting with a hideous-looking Arab, throwing back her head and laughing at his feeble jokes. The overweight sand-nigger kept taking huge bundles of money from a Louis Vuiton suitcase and setting them on fire, much to the Princess's girlish amusement.

"So Rod," I said, draining a glass of two grand a bottle champagene, "Balfe tells me you're interested in working with us." I continued checking out the major rock biz philanthropist, kind, caring man of rock's aura.

"Yes Z, that's right," he answered, looking me earnestly in the eye. "Both myself and my partner Mr Taylor here are not evil in the slightest." He indicated his dignified-looking partner who added, "Yes and although I'm Jewish I can assure you Mr Mindwarp sir that I have never ritually slaughtered a gentile child in my entire life." Elie seemed earnest and I almost believed him.

"Dave tells me that you have one or two other bands under your wing," I continued with the formal chit-chat. The Hundred Pipers whiskey had arrived so I knew things would probably start to liven up a little later.

"Yes that's right Zodiac. As you know we do a lot of charitable work which brings us into contact with many seriously underprivileged and mentally handicapped children, which is why we decided to help a few of them in the ways that we know best," continued Rod seriously, "Are you familiar with the band Iron Mongol?" he asked. I was, they were one of the best Mongol Rock bands on the planet.

"Iron Mongol?" said Cobalt, spitting out a piece of fricaséed monkey bumhole. "You manage Iron Mongol? Fuck man, they're one of my favourite Mongol Rock bands ever, the guitarist, Downy Syndrome, man that cat rocks! Bring your Mongol daughter to the slaughter? 666, the number of the Mongol? Man, Iron Mongol rule!" exclaimed the Stargazer, genuinely impressed.

"We also have an interest in Guns and Mongols," added Rod with a slightly smug tilt of his head.

"Welcome to the Mongol baby!" sang Cobalt, "Guns and Mongols, fucking hell man! Mongl Pose what a singer! And the guitarist, whats his name? The little three-foot guy with the top hat, looks like one of Ken Dodd's diddymen? Piss! That's him, cool man, Take me down to Paradise city, where the mongol girls are all so pretty, ooooh yeaah, let me take you mongol, mongol, mongol yeah!" shouted Cobalt leaping onto his chair and peeling off an air-mongol guitar solo.

"Yes I thought you'd be impressed, I find mongols are a very musical people," added the philanthropist manager who wasn't evil at all, and whose partner definitely didn't ritually slaughter children at Easter.

Of course Balfe got us a fantastic deal.

Rod and Elie would manage us, get us gigs and record deals and they wouldn't charge us a penny because they were such kind and nice people and they thought that we were very talented and handsome.

The deal was that when we did gigs and made records they would give us as much beer as we could drink and as many monkeynuts as we could eat.

What great guys. Balfe never gave us free beer and peanuts.

We set off to conquer America.

"Man that Rod guy's fucking cool isn't he?" said Slam eating a Roy Rogers

triple cheese burger that he had got for free off of Rod and Elie.

"They're both of them the nicest people I've ever met," replied Cobalt, decking a free can of beer.

"Yeah," I added, "And the Jewish one says he's never ritually slaughtered a child in his life," I said confidently.

"Did you see Rod's house man, wasn't it cool?" Slam again.

"I've never seen so many half-naked handicapped kids swimming and enjoying themselves in my life," commented the Stargazer ripping off another ringpull.

"Man we are so lucky to have such a great management team."

Because Rod and Elie were such big shots over in the States we didn't really have to play any of the shitty toilet gigs. Our first gig on American soil was as support for those kings of Mongol Rock, Guns and Mongols.

In Britain the largest show we'd ever done was Reading, sixty thousand drunken headbangers rolling around in a big field of mud and throwing bottles of piss at the bands.

We thought that was a fuck-sized gig but it was nothing compared to the Humongoldrome.

The Humongoldrome was a converted ice hockey stadium and had a maximum capacity of two hundred thousand.

Two hundred thousand rocked-out mongols man, fucking incredible.

Mongol Rock was and still is massive in America and at the time Guns and Mongols, along with Aeromongol and Iron Mongol, were probably the biggest acts around.

Despite their popularity and obvious mental handicaps the Guns and Mongols guys were pretty cool, I mean they didn't act like big stars or anything. Piss, the three-foot-tall guitarist with the top hat got pretty friendly with Cobalt, which I guess is where our relationship with Rod and Elie first started to deteriorate.

I mean if Cobalt hadn't have been so friendly with the fucking little dwarf he would never have seen inside of Piss's dressing room and well, what you don't know, if you know what I mean.

"Those fucking spastic-shagging, childfuckingmolesting bastards!" shouted the furious guitarist as he kicked open the dressing room door and punched a hole in the toilet. I could tell Cobalt was super angry as he had started putting swear words in between words, this is a very special skill and only people who are really good at swearing can absofuckinglutely do this.

"Calm down Cobalt, fucking hell man I was just going to have a shit," said Slam, surveying the karate-shattered shitter.

"Yeah man, easy tiger, what's the problem?" I said.

"I knew they were a couple of bastards, where's the phone, I'm gonna call those ritual murderers right this minute," spat the furious karate expert toilet-smashing guitarist through gritted teeth.

"What Rod and Elie, don't be stupid, they'd never ritually murder a child or have sex with mentally handicapped children," I said nervously.

"Oh no?" shot Cobalt provocatively. "Well you should see what I've just fucking seen, bastards!"

"What? What have you seen Cobalt?" said Slam wiping his arse, he'd shat on the toilet floor and covered it up with a towel.

"In Guns and Mongols' dressing room r, r, right," he stuttered, boiling with emotion and pointing at the ceiling. "They've got like fucking, fucking shitshit fucking fucking loads of fucking b, b ,b, beer!" Cobalt's anger had now started to swirl around the Tourettes Syndrome end of rage.

"Yeah, and so have we," answered Slam pointing at the twenty crates each of Tennants Super that we had on the rider for each gig, still unsure why Johhnny karate was so wound up.

"Fucking, fucking monkey fucking shitting nuts..." He was starting to have problems communicating at all now, so incandescant was his rage. Usually when Cobalt reaches this stage of mania rage he stops using ordinary words completely and is just caught up in a maelstrom of profanity, a whirling dervish of bad language. A torfuckingnado of swearing.

"Yeah?" Slam again, pointing at the tin bath full of Percy Daltons that we had backstage at every gig.

"And fucking, fucking, fucking, shit, cunt, wank, bollocks, fuck, fuck, fuck, fuck.."

It looked like the Tourettes had got him.

"Come on Cobalt, you can do it," teased Slam. "Take a deep breath."

"They've got fucking cashew nuts as well!" Cobalt managed to blurt out. "And fucking, fucking, fucking PISTACHIOS!!!" he screamed, kicking over our tin bath full of peanuts. A dread silence filled the room. This was serious, that Smallwood cunt and his sidekike were taking the piss.

"They've got pistachios as well?" said Slam. "Are you sure?"

"Of course I'm fucking sure, I saw them! Sat in their little split shells, a whole fucking tin bath full of the green little fuckers!" said Cobalt coughing now, tears welling at the corners of his eyes.

"Shit man, and I thought those guys were on the level, the bastards." Slam shook his head resignedly. "Man I bet fucking Iron Mongol get choclate coated peanuts," he added. "In fact I bet they get candy coated chocolate fucking peanuts man, I bet they get fucking M&M's!" he concluded, stamping angrily on the scattered nuts.

"And little mongol birds!" Cobalt shouted. "About thirty of them, all running around in little bikinis doing blowjobs and being bummed by anyone who wants to bum them!"

"Hello Rod?" said Slam into the phone, we all stopped what we were doing and listened. "No, it's well, actually it is important yes, you're in a meeting?" he continued.

"Fucking give me that phone," butted in Cobalt, grabbing at the cellular. "Listen man, I've just been in Guns and Mongols' dressing room right and.... what? Really? No no it wasn't important, cool, OK yeah see you in L.A., great, right, excellent..." Cobalt pressed the button and turned around smiling. "Pistachios, cashews, almonds and McDonalds, Dominos and Taco Bell. Round here in about ten minutes with about forty Thai mongol massage birds. Yes!!!" laughed the happy man. "The promotor fucked up, Rod's been sorting it out all morning, apparantly our mongol birds are much better than Guns and Mongols' little slappers, ha ha, yes, The Love Reaction triumph again." Cobalt cracked open a fresh can of purple liver stench and we toasted our good fortune and fantasticity once more.

The tour of course was a great success. Selling out venues all across the East and West Coast and the majority of the Mid West. Our records charted in Billboard and we were hailed as the new kings of Mongol Rock in America.

So you can imagine our surprise when we got back to England with our rucksacks bursting with cashews and pistachios to find all our homes repossessed.

We tried to track down Balfe but he'd moved to a big castle in another country and we couldn't find him.

When we tried to get in touch with our great American friends and managers we were given the curt and simple instruction to go and fuck ourselves.

ZEDIAC

"Are there any peanuts left Slam?" said Cobalt.

"No and that's the last can of Tennants as well, so don't fucking drink it all," snapped the stinking drunk hide-thrasher, his head wobbling back and forward.

"Here have one of mine, I've got a couple," I said pulling the last two remaining cans of Tennants Super from my Tescos carrier bag.

We were sat on the little wall just outside Camden tube station with a bunch of other guys who had failed to crack America.

"Itsss all fuckinn bloccks" slurred Arse Cider, ex-lead guitarist with The Bumfuckers before throwing a huge arc of watery vomit across his legs and falling sideways onto the street. "Fuckin 'Merica!" said Bladder, the ex-bass player from Dire Shite, razzling off a wet one. "Fucking cider" he added angrily standing up in his diarrhoea-stained pants and stumbling off bow-legged to try and find somewhere to clean himself up. "Come on," said Cobalt standing up unsteadily. "Grab that cunt." He pointed at Slam, who had fallen asleep amongst all the styrofoam cups, empty Tennants cans, dog shit, fag ends and other tramps. "Let's go to Europe."

I picked up my bum drummer friend, heaved him across my shoulder and set off with Cobalt to see if we could find a big silver tourbus anywhere.

TESTOSTERONE TORNADO
DRAMATIS PERSONAE #1: SMITHY

"What the fuck's that?" said Slam, turning down the sound on the *Mortal Kombat* video game.

"For fuck's sake Slam!" screamed Cobalt, "I'm just about to get fucking Goro down!" We were all sat in the vampire ambience of the tourbus back lounge. It was only mid-day but it could have been anytime in the universe, as Cobalt had taped all the curtains shut.

Cobalt was sat there, the king of the undead in his black German porno star jockey briefs and his sunglasses, surrounded by avalanching ashtrays and crushed beer cans.

Empty vodka bottles and Jack Daniels bottles littered the floor like icebergs in a polluted sea of dirty, skidmark underpants and dirtier, stinkier socks.

Suzy X, comatose from his continued efforts at smoking all the marijuana on earth lay dribbling in a corner, we'd propped him upright so that he wouldn't choke if he puked while he was away with the elves of Spliffland.

"No man listen," shouted Slam again. "What the fuck is it? It sounds like somebody locked in a fucking trunk or something," he went on.

"Oh yeah man, listen Cobalt, what is it?" I said.

There was some kind of muffled shouting-type sound and banging coming from somewhere, as if there was someone locked underneath the bus or something.

"It's coming from down there," said Slam pointing to the aisle down the centre of the bus where all our bunks were. "Look!" he shouted "There's something kicking the curtains on Smithy's bunk."

Sure enough, the flimsy curtain that was the only privacy we had on these rolling barnyards was flapping away. "Shall I check it out?" he asked.

One of the few rules we had on the bus was that you respected a man's bunk, didn't go snooping around when he wasn't there, trying to find bizarre tug or any other weird shit with which to taunt him.

Tempers became frayed enough on the road without the added tensions brought about by commenting and mocking another man's sordid wank fantasies.

But this was different, there seemed to be something alive in there.

Slam walked gingerly down the aisle and gently pulled back the curtain,

GIMPO

Archbishop of Bashington, scars on the love pump, dirtbox invader Gimpo the Impaler, semen-spattered Tasmanian Devil, whirling wanking dervish, idiot savant with ants in his pants, Gimpo Lord of the Underworld, Sigmund Freud's jack-in-the-box nightmare auto rapist.

SMITHY

Dark dreams in Disneyland and Teddybears in Vietnam, oilstains and motorway curses, apocalypse this morning, broken alarm clocks and no vegetables, army surplus dandy with a beer-stained baseball cap, blood-knot arse destroyer, frightened guitars and roses for girls.

MARK MANNING

before bursting out laughing and running down the aisle.

"Fuck man, there's some fucking bird in there, all tied up and gagged!" he whispered loudly. "She's got no fucking clothes on either!"

"What?" Said Cobalt, pressing pause on his Nintendo.

We walked down the aisle and pulled open the curtain. "Fucking hell!" said the Stargazer. "She doesn't look very happy," he added.

She didn't.

The poor girl looked close to a state of panic, she was wriggling and trying to scream something, but you couldn't hear what she was saying because of the gag.

"Maybe we should take the gag off? It looks like she's trying to tell us something," I suggested.

"No way man," said Slam. "Smithy would go fucking apeshit if he found out you'd been fucking around with his bird."

"Yeah but look Slam," I said, slightly concerned, "She looks like she's in pain, her arse is bleeding man look." A dark trickle of blood was leaking down the back of her legs and staining the grubby sheets on Smithy's bunk. What had the rotten bastard done to her?

"You fucking take it off man, I'm not fucking going near her," repeated the cautious skin-thumper.

"Cobalt, take off the gag man, see what the poor cunt wants," I urged the guitarist, reluctant to do it myself.

Slam was right.

Smithy did have a ferocious temper and anything could set it off.

We all kind of knew instinctively that the humongo biker would be well pissed off if he caught us messing around with his trussed up little fuckpiggy. The girl started screaming under the gag and wriggling, her eyes stretched wide open, filling up with tears, kind of like pleading with us or something.

"Fuck it man, she might need to go to the toilet or something," I said. "I'm going to untie her gag."

I tried undoing the knot, it took fucking ages, Smithy had used some weird sailor's type knot on it.

"Oh God!" coughed the girl as I eventually got the damn thing off. "Get Smithy quick for fuck's sake!" she gasped, "I need to get to the hospital quickly, my fucking arse is falling out."

Smithy was always doing this.

Tying women up, buggering their lungs out and then forgetting all about them. You'd open up a flight case and there'd be some bound and gagged little Sheila wriggling like a nude caterpillar, blood and shit running all down the back of her legs.

You'd come offstage after a gig and there would be another one hidden away in the shower stall.

I'm surprised he never killed any of them.

The thing is, you always had to get him to untie his little trussed up turkeys because of the knots.

Some of the knots he used were incredible.

Apparently as a lad he was a Sea Scout and that's where he learned all about slippery hitches, tom fools, blood knots and all manner of other nautical sliding rope magic.

To say The Smith was an odd sod would be putting it mildly.

His penchant for violent SM Bondage and domination buggery sex was one of the more normal things about our Biker monster guitar tech.

Smithy was a lot like Gimpo in one respect – although he'd probably brain me for saying there was even one thing similar about him and the Gimp.

Gimpo and Smithy were sworn enemies and hated each other with a vengeance. Actually there were several things similar about them come to think of it.

Both of them liked bumming women to within an inch of their lives, both of them had foul tempers, both were extremely violent and both of them had been in the army.

And this fact, I think, is where the mutual animosity lay.

Some kind of hierarchical military sodomistic weirdness thing.

Gimpo had been an ordinary squaddie whilst Smith had been part of an elite. The Royal Marines.

This was not all though, if it had been merely a rank and hierarchy thing it would have been simple, Smithy would have been top sausage.

No contest, Frankie Frankfurter my friend.

But in the macho hell that is the world of an ex-member of Her Majesty's collection of target-practice goon squads, things had been made more complicated by the fact that Gimpo had seen combat.

Not only had Gimpo seen combat however, it had been of a particular kind.

Real gruesome, beheading, disembowelling, raping, triple gory, soldier

101

bumming, Goose Green-type combat in the Falklands.

Even more complicated however was the fact that after qualifying as a fully fledged, running fifty miles carrying a lump of concrete, climbing up a mountain clenching a cannon between your bumcheeks Marine, the Smithster had been kicked out.

Deep shame on his family.

All the men in the Smith family had been Royal Marines ever since Wellington singlehandedly carrried a cannon all the way to Waterloo clenched between his bumcheeks. Sergeant's stripes ripped off, buttons ripped off, sword broken in half, *Branded*-type vibe with Chuck Connors, that kind of thing.

Now as a band we all thought that decking an officer was far cooler than obeying orders and having a bunch of strangers throw fire and bombs at you like the Gimp did.

I mean, telling a CO to go fuck himself and whacking him on the parade ground in front of all the men, that took a certain amount of bollocks and style.

But not in the Smithster's eyes, in some strange way he felt slightly ashamed, somehow thought that he had failed at being a Marine, which he didn't, he passed out the fucking works, he just had this little – how shall we put it – discipline problem.

"I just can't take orders," he said one night tearfully after nineteen million Jack Daniels, as if this was something to be ashamed of.

Like I say, a strange fucker.

I mention all of this as it seems to be about one of the only ways to understand the incredible amount of insane, angry machismo Smithy trailed in his wake like a tornado of testosterone.

I mean it wasn't just his threatening manner, threatening to kill without exception every single member of all the support acts, their crews, management and friends that we ever played with.

That was quite funny, seeing grown singers pissing their leather trousers like little girls, it was all the other stuff that was weird.

I mean Smithy could not do anything, and I mean, anything, without maximum force and some imminent threat of murder and death lurking in the corner.

I mean even his eating habits were macho.

"I don't fucking eat vegetables," he growled, picking out the gherkins from his quarterpounder in a McDonalds shithole and throwing them aggressively at some acned Saturday job, school kid table wiper.

"What none at all Smith," said Slam, smiling apologetically as the poor youngster fished the offending gherkin out of his eye.

"None," he grunted, centre of attention, which I suspect was the real reason for this explanation of his bizarre affectation.

"What not like even sprouts or anything?" said Kid Chaos, intrigued.

"Are you taking the piss?" snapped the paranoid carnivore.

"God no," added Kid Chaos. "I wouldn't dare, all I meant was like, you don't eat any at all? You don't just not eat saladdy girly things, like lettuce and cucumbers, you mean you don't even eat manly vegetables like potatoes and parsnips either?" he continued, digging his grave even deeper.

"Manly vegetables?" snarled the biker flesh eater. "Are you questioning my sexual orientation you fag??" Smithy added, throwing a slice of inedible processed McDonalds cheese at Kid. "I just eat fucking meat alright! Fucking vegetables make you weak!"

Somehow cheese came into the fag category as well.

Smithy ate the weirdest pizzas.

No cheese or tomatoes, just salami and ham and ground beef.

He obviously had the angriest bowel syndrome in the world.

Playing pool, bowling, swimming, everything was done with maximum aggression.

He would break at a game of pool, pulling back his meaty arm and ramming the balls with all his might, a mighty crack resounding around the bar, deafening anyone within five foot of the table, balls turning to chalkdust.

Around the baize he would stalk like a grizzly bear, pulling back his hickory and grunting like a pig as he jabbed at the white ball as if it were a mortal enemy.

He would thunder down bowling alley aisles like a Sherman tank hurling the heaviest bowls in the place as if they were cannonballs out to sink the spanish Armada. Skittles smashing all over the fucking place like incendiary bombs.

And swimming.

How the fuck do you do macho aggressive swimming?

You should see Smithy do the crawl. He thought we were all fags because we did the breast stroke.

For Smithy a gig wasn't a pleasant experience. It was some kind of war, a military operation where we, the band were going over the top and the audience were the enemy.

"Ride Of The Valkyries" (Smithy's choice). The martial piece of Wagnerian opera that features in Smithy's favourite film of all time, *Apocalypse Now,* would be blaring out of the PA system. "Ride Of The Valkyries" was our intro tape. Me, Cobalt, Slam and Kid Chaos would be crouching in the wings, lights flashing, smoke billowing and Smithy shouting at us as if we were in the trenches in World War One. "Wait a minute!! Down Cobalt down!! Z get back! Get back!! Chaos DOWNDOWNDOWN! OK! 5, 4, 3, TURN THAT FUCKING LIGHT OFF!!! 2! 1! GO! GO! GO!"

And then we would run onstage terrified that we were about to be mown down by the Hun, strafed by enemy fighters. But of course all that awaited us was a hall of overexcited teenagers who were overjoyed to see us.

Of course all this macho insanity leaked into the other areas of Smithy's life, which is why none of us liked sharing a room with him.

I only shared once. Never again. I think I'd rather share a room with Fred West than share with Smithy ever again.

We had inklings about the Smithster's *recherché* sexual predilictions not only from the trussed-up girls we kept finding all over the place but once when we accidentally pried open his personal flight case and came across all his equipment.

Huge bottle of industrial strength Rohypnol, the famous date rape drug. Handcuffs, rope, knives, special gags, weird gynaecological-type instruments and all kinds of weird rubber shit we didn't understand.

It was about four in the morning – I'd hit my coma about an hour earlier – when I was awakened by some kind of slurred screaming. I thought I was dreaming but noticed that the bathroom light was on and there were these weird sounds coming from in there. A girl kind of pleading and this horrible guttural growling sound. Suddenly the unmistakeable sound of a huge piece of gaffa being ripped of a roll. The screams became muffled and I could hear metal.

I got up and went to explore. Maybe Slam and Cobalt were fucking around in there, they often fucked around in bathrooms making things and writing rock operas.

Jesus I wish I hadn't.

There he was.

The sex beast monster of the Apocalypse.

Bollock naked, like a huge silverback gorilla except for a full face leather mask with a zip where the mouth should be. Some young girl was chained to the shower rail with all kinds of horrible things sticking out of her arse. Smithy had a knife and fork in his hands, he looked at me and screamed at me to get out.

He didn't have to say it twice.

I ran down the hall to Cobalt and Slam's room and started banging on the door, scared he was going to come after me with his Rohypnol and knife and fork.

Of course at breakfast the next day, the Smith tucked into his bacon and bacon as if nothing had happened. His little breakfast partner, while missing a couple of front teeth and heavily bruised about the face, looked happy enough so none of us said anything.

No-one knows what eventually happened to The Smith.

He just disappeared.

Cobalt reckons he had to go into hiding after pissing off The Satans Rats motorcycle club over something or other. Slam reckons him and Joe set up a brothel in Thailand.

There have been more sightings of the Smith than Lord Lucan and Gary Glitter put together.

But I know where the motorcycle madman is hanging out.

And for the first time I can reveal it right here.

Smithy has opened a hotel for Transvestites in Devon.

A relaxing place where men can get in touch with the feminine sides of their personalities.

Ian's Devonshire Chi Chi Lounge it's called.

How do I know?

Bill Drummond, who is very in touch with the feminine side of his nature and a keen cross dresser, told me. He came across the advert for it in *Transvestite Times* and although he calls himself Simona these days, Bill swears that the big guy in the mauve housecoat with matching fluffy mules was none other than the Smithster himself.

So there you have it.

MARK MANNING

There is hope for the world after all.

If Smithy can find the courage to throw of all the baggage of his terrible military upbringing and truly be himself, then there's no reason the rest of us can't be true to ourselves.

God bless you Simona, wherever you are.

You are an inspiration to us all.

A BUCKET OF PISS

We were recording demos for our first album on Cosmosodomistic Records.
At the Manor.
Demos.
The Manor.
The Manor is Richard Branson's mega, residential, luxury, spoilt rock star bastard recording studios, and we were doing demos there.
I mean, like where were we going to record the real thing? Buckingham fucking Palace?
So as you can imagine we were all suffering from major hubris – that's like posh for big-headed – had been for weeks, ever since we signed our souls over to those kind people at the record company.
It was the first real money any of us had ever had in our entire lives.
Fifty quid notes flew around like confetti in the wake of our stretch limos as we dashed from nightclub to nightclub.
Peter Stringfellow was our best mate.
Champagne and lap dancers rained down from the sky wherever we went.
The world was our donut and we were going to fuck it up the arse.
And being intelligent musicians we decided of course, that because we were so important, great and famous, we had better upgrade our birds.
We all four of us got rid of the kind, selfless, loving women who we had met when we were penniless nobodies.
Kind, selfless, loving women who had loved us for who we were and not because we were in some stupid band.
Who supported us and cared for us all through the hard times.
Who went hungry so that we could have extra large fries with our Big Macs and Burger Kings.
Who washed our leather trousers and darned our underpants.
Who lovingly polished our guitars with breast grease and carried our amplifiers to gigs for us.
Who took extra jobs as cleaners so we could afford new strings for every performance.
Who would tuck us up in bed and bring us cups of hot Jack Daniels.
Who would hose us down after we drank too much and shat ourselves.
Who would sleep on the floor at the side of the bed so we could be more

comfortable.

Who gave us sex whenever we wanted it.

Who fellated us kindly through the long dark nights of our souls, which seemed to be every weekend.

Who would let us savagely bum them and even pretend to like it.

Kind, decent, loving women who wanted nothing more than to have our babies, raise a family and bake bread in a little house on the prairie.

We got rid of all those stupid ugly bitches and got in a rake of hot models, porn actresses, strippers, posh blondes and record company sluts.

Fucking right we did, what do you think we were? Stupid or something?

Wise guys, that was us.

Well, me and Cobalt were, never looked back once.

Got rid of our long-suffering wives and moved on into the happy gash valley.

Banging and buggering, shagging and torturing, murdering and raping like there was no tomorrow.

Porn stars, Page 3 birds, strippers, little schoolgirls, posh bitches, the fucking lot. I'm surprised our fucking cocks didn't fall off.

Kid Chaos didn't fuck around either, he was banging his way through half the professional rock chick sluts in London.

No band's girlfriends were safe when their prize turkeys went away on tour.

He left a wake of spunky devastation all the way from the St Moritz metal toilet in Soho to the grand, white-painted rock star mansions of West London.

It was Slam who came down with slut ennui first of all.

Right there in the Manor.

Of course he'd made the effort, dumped his wife and moved on to the London rock slag scene, banging his way through the PR floozies and press department shagbags of just about every record company in Europe.

But Slam had started to miss his wife.

Started getting sentimental when he realised that he might have made a terrible mistake.

Maybe he should have stuck with his childhood sweetheart who he had married when they were both eighteen over in Canada?

What was he doing with these hard-hearted record company whores?

These spandex-clad, suspender-wearing fellatrixes who sucked the sperm out of anything in leather trousers.

He was right of course.

And he knew it.

I was sitting around in the TV lounge one night watching a porno film with a couple of spunkburpers who were actually in the fucking thing, one of them was sucking me off, the other was passed out on the settee next to me, I had my entire hand up her arse, when I noticed Slam peering in through the patio window.

I waved him inside and asked him if he wanted to bugger one of the girls or anything.

The drummer looked sort of sad, as if he'd been crying or something. "No it's alright Z, I've just anally raped one of Cobalt's girlfriends, Kid Chaos is banging her now, I'm leaving, it's been great knowing you," replied the strange drummer, turning around and leaving through the patio doors.

He tripped and fell face first into the mud.

I heard him curse as he wandered into the dark.

I didn't really think anything more about it, the cunt was obviously pissed and he was always saying weird shit when he was drunk.

The next afternoon I was having breakfast with Cobalt when I noticed a pad with what looked like Slam's spiky, barely legible handwriting. "That's not what I think it is, is it Cobalt?" I said to the hungry guitarist, pointing to the pad at his elbow.

Cobalt pushed the girl who was fellating him beneath the table angrily away. "Will you just leave my cock alone for two fucking minutes, you filthy fucking bitch!" he snapped, zipping his cock up and picking up the pad. He scanned the short note quickly and nodded. "I'm afraid so, another one," he said resignedly.

"Why's he going to kill himself this time?" I groaned, it was obviously another of Slam's suicide notes.

"Dear Z, Cobalt, Kid I'm sorry blah blah, usual shit na, na, I've made a terrible mistake, blah, blah Cathy, nah nah I can't go on, tell her I'm sorry na, na, na, signed Slam. The usual fucking crap, ragging on about his ex-Mrs and that record company cocksucker he's been boning," said the heartless guitarist.

"Have you seen him this morning?" I said.

"No I haven't actually, why you don't think he's gone and done it do you?" said Cobalt incredulously.

MARK MANNING

"I don't know man, he was in a fucking weird mood last night," I replied, remembering his funny little speech in the TV lounge. "I'll go and see if he's in his room."

I wandered into suicide boy's room and found him lying on the floor.

There was a piece of string round his neck and a broken lightbulb next to his naked arse.

The idiot had obviously tried to hang himself from the light fittings. "Slam," I said, shaking him. "Wake up you arsehole." I noticed the empty whiskey bottle under the bed. "You've ballsed it up again. You're alive you twat."

The hungover bad suicide boy groaned, realised what he had been up to the previous night and reached for the empty bottle. "Shit," he grunted, "Not again."

"You're going to have to be careful Slam man," I said to the hungover failed self-topper. "You might fucking just pull it off one of these days."

"That's the whole goddamn point you fucking asshole, do you think I want to keep fucking up my suicides," he shouted, realising that he was still pretty much on his mortal coil.

"I don't know man. It just seems like every other day Cobalt or myself find you like, drunk in the dustbin of another failed suicide attempt," I said remembering the electric fire in the bath, that wasn't plugged in. The eight thousand sweetex he'd taken, the leap from the top of a bungalow, the list went on. "I mean are you unhappy or something Slam?" I added concernedly.

"Am I upset?!" he shouted, tears of confused rage welling in his bloodshot eyes. "My whole life's been flushed down the goddamn toilet, I'm living with a whore, my beautiful loving wife who I've known since childhood I treated like a groupie! Am I upset!?" The emotional drummer reached around his neck for the piece of string and threw it cursorily away. "Can't fucking hang yourself with a piece of fucking string," he mumbled, placing his head in his hands and shaking it slowly from side to side.

I managed to persuade him to come downstairs and have a little breakfast.

The handsome Canadian helped himself to a boiled egg and a large refreshing vodka.

"So Slammy, what's it this time?" said helpful Cobalt, sounding completely unconcerned, as if Slam was just suffering from a hangover and not another botched suicide attempt.

"You know what it is Cobalt," said Slam as surly as a tomcat after his snip-trip to the vet's.

"What, not the ex-bitch, again?"

"She's my ex-wife Cobalt, and she's not a bitch."

"Sorry, sorry," protested Cobalt, holding up his hands defensively.

"She's beautiful, she's kind, she loves me – loved me," said our distressed friend, wiping away a tear with the back of his hand. "For who I am. Not like the sluts you three have been banging for the past year! God what have I done..." The drummer slung back his refreshing vodka and poured himself another.

"For fuck's sake Slam," said Cobalt, helping himself to a refreshing vodka himself. "Why don't you just try getting back with her instead of all this crap suicide shit, just fucking call her." He continued filling up Slam's glass with yet another refreshing vodka.

"She'd never have me back, not after what I did. I broke her poor innocent heart, she was a virgin you know," said the Slamster. "Innocent child, love of my life, she pressed flowers and loved rabbits, springtime was her favourite time of the year. She would dance amongst crocuses, I thought she was an angel who had somehow lost her memory, fallen from heaven and couldn't remember where she came from." Slam wiped away another tear, and poured another refreshing voddy.

"Just call her up, ask her out for a date or something, just as friends, you know the routine, see if there's anything worth salvaging," smiled cynical old Stargazer, the master of bitch psychology.

I just groaned.

"You think so Cobalt?" said the hopelessly romantic idiot. "Yeah you could be right, all casual, just a drink or something, yeah Cobalt, thanks man, I'm going to call her right now!" Slam leapt up from the breakfast table, spilling his sixth refreshing breakfast vodka and knocking over his chair.

Ten minutes later a new man sprinted back into the breakfast room. "Saturday man!" he beamed. "I just spoke to Kathy, I'm going round and we're going out for a meal. She seemed really pleased to hear from me. You know I think if I play my cards right and everything, maybe?.." It was nice to see Slam happy again, for the previous six months it had been like rocking with Dr Doom.

Four days later and Saturday came.

MARK MANNING

Slam had been in the bath all morning polishing his bollocks and oiling up his bell-end. He ironed his leathers and cleaned the soles of his engineer boots.

His beard looked as if it had been drawn on his chin with Indian ink, so neatly sculpted was his tonsorial elegance.

"How do I look?" said the nervous sticksman, on his way to woo back his lady love.

Yeah cool, seemed to be the general consensus of his three rocking compadres.

The nervous Slam ordered flowers from Interflora to be delivered to his ex-wife's, and set off for the railway station.

About midnight the same day we found Slam with his head in the oven.

"Slam," said Cobalt to Slam's arse. "It's an electric oven."

"Fuck off!" came the echoing reply.

"It's not even turned on," added the bemused guitarist.

"Fuck off! again.

"What are you trying to do? Bake yourself to death?"

Slam pulled himself out of the oven and sat surlily at the table. Vodka. And tonic.

"So what happened?" I asked Johnny useless-suicide. Fucking electric oven, Jesus.

"I pretty much think she wasn't interested," said Slam, chucking it back in one.

"What do you mean? Is that what she said? What happened?" said Cobalt a little too enthusiastically.

"You're really enjoying this Stargazer aren't you? You fucking bastard," spat Slam, heaving another monster shot into his bucket glass.

"No I'm not!" lied Cobalt, the terminal soap opera fan.

"Well I got there, all excited and everything, you know," said Slam.

"Yeah?" Cobalt again.

"And like I ring the doorbell, you know waiting for the window to open on the first floor and for her to throw down the key," continued lover boy.

"And?"

"She threw a bucket of piss all over me."

As you can imagine we all just creased up, laughing like maniacs.

"I knew you bastards would think it was funny. God, how did I ever get

involved with such a bunch of insensitive bastards as you lot?" said Slam, disgusted at his friends.

"What like a full bucket?" asked Kid Chaos between belly laughs.

"Yeah man, the fucking bitch must have been pissing in it ever since I made that fucking phone call," added Slam, a little incredulous at how his sweet bunny-loving ex had crouched down for over four days preparing this little liquid rebuttal to his request for some kind of marital reconciliation.

"Man, it could have been worse," said Cobalt all concerned.

"Oh yeah," said Slam. "Like how worse can a bucket of piss on your head be. I was stood there man, with like a little box of chocolates, not cheap ones either man, they were like Terry's All Gold man, you know what I'm saying?" said Slammy all hurt.

"Well, she could have shat in the bucket for four days as well," guffawed his sympathetic guitarist friend.

Slam laughed, reluctantly. "Fucking cunt," he said, chuckling.

He was alright.

I'M GOING TO TELL THE FEMINISTS

"What did she say?" said Cobalt, pushing some sprightly young groupie off his cock.

"That she's going to tell the feminists," I said, pausing my own little blow jobber, mid-nosh.

We were backstage at JB's in Dudley, that top notch Midlands rocking club, taking drugs and having sex with underage girls.

Some semi-naked floozy had just sprinted out of the toilet rearranging her bra and banging on about grassing us up to the feminists.

"Fucking hell, sounds scary," said Cobalt. "What are feminists anyway, are they like the police or something?" he continued, fastening Lolita back onto his bell-end.

"Sort of," I replied, flipping schoolgirl on her belly and jamming it up her jacksie.

"I mean they'd like to be, but really they're just a bunch of pissed-off cunts that wish they'd been born with dicks."

Slam came out of the toilet fastening up his flies.

"What was all that shit man?" said Cobalt, jizzing down the throat of his little Jodie Kidd lookalike.

"Fuck knows man, fucking cunt started bollocking on about female orgasms and stuff, fucking crazy," answered the drummer, cracking a beer.

'What's a female orgasm?" said Cobalt.

"I think it's like when chicks jizz, except that they don't kind of, something like that anyway," I said unconcerned.

"Weird," said Cobalt.

We pretty much forgot about the incident.

Shit like this was always happening.

Female hysteria, PMS we put it down to.

That or something else equally bizarre, female and weird.

But then the bitches turned up.

Fucking feminists.

Arggghhh!

I mean, what are these monsters? They're not women, and they're not men. They're not even transvestites.

The door flew open and this bunch of ragged women, angry as fuck, came

barging into the small dressing room. "Put that woman down immediately!" said one of the feminists.

Obviously the boss, well lippy.

She wasn't bad looking actually, for a mentally ill person, that is.

I mean if she'd combed her hair, a little lipstick maybe, high heels, she would probably have looked half-decent.

Well, decent enough for old Texy boy to fuck – but I wouldn't have gone near it.

"What, this?" said Cobalt, pulling little Spunkalina from his bell-end and holding her gingerly by the ears.

"That's him!" said the young girl I'd seen running from the toilet earlier. She was pointing accusingly at Slam.

"What the fuck have I done?" said the hapless drummer, as if fannybatter wouldn't melt in his mouth.

"It's more what you haven't done, you patriarchal bastard!" denounced the lippy one. She was obviously the feminists' leader. About twenty-seven, she looked like some kind of post-graduate media studies imbecile, media studies or some other equally useless shite.

She obviously read the *Guardian* women's section and took it seriously, the idiotic cunt. "Our sister Germaine here says that, that, that man..." she pointed at Slam, her lips curling in contempt at Mr Thunderhide, "Failed to satisfy her sexually, giving her neither a clitoral nor a vaginal orgasm."

"What the fuck are you talking about you insane bitch?" laughed Slam, standing up and swaggering casually towards the quaking harridan.

"What's a clitoral orgasm?" said Cobalt once more, confused.

His little Spunkalina shrugged her shoulders and carried on working the guitarist's stinkhorn, she didn't seem to know either.

"Don't come near me you rapist!" spat boss feminist at Slam.

"In your fucking dreams lesbo!" quipped Slam. "What's wrong with you fucking bitches anyway, are you all on the fucking rag this week or something?" he continued.

A few of the shyer looking feminists blushed, you could tell that they all fancied the devastatingly handsome Canadian drummer. "Why are you all so uptight, here have a fucking beer, Jesus." A couple of the girls reached out to take a drink from Slam.

"Don't!" screamed out the boss Fem. "He's trying to get you drunk so he can rape you, he wants to lick your vaginas and feel your breasts, wants to ram his big rock star cock in your cunts and keep banging and banging and banging and banging, ramming it into you, he wants to stick his pulsating manhood in your mouth, he wants to ejaculate his horrible big fat thing into your face, he wants to... Oh God you bastard come here!"

The Boss Fem grabbed hold of Slam and pulled him to the ground.

Never one to look a gift feminist in the fanny, Slam started banging her one up the arse. Feminist oberfuhrer started moaning like an American. "You macho bastard," she groaned, obviously loving it.

The other feminists were obviously getting turned on by the little floor show and before you knew it they were down on their knees sucking on mine, Tex's and Cobalt's knobs.

I pulled little Germaine off my cock and flung her up on her knees, ramming it into her from behind. "Oh yes, rape me you fucking stud," she moaned "I, like all feminists, have wild insane rape fantasies all the time. Whenever I take a ride on my fifteen-inch donkey kong dildo I always fantasise about being raped by a troop of beery gorillas on motorcycles. I hate feminism!" moaned my slut, writhing around on the gristlehammer.

"Yes, me too," mumbled some other feminist between gulps of Cobalt's sperm.

"Well that doesn't really surprise me girls," I said, still banging hard on my teenager's ringpiece. "You see you've all been duped into believing some bogus crackpot theory thought up in the late sixties and early seventies by a bunch of bitter man-hating ugly old bags who have never had a decent shag in their entire lives and for some weird reason think somehow that there's this bizarre conspiracy of men called Patriarchs denying them all the super orgasms that they've read about in women's magazines."

Little Germaine was squirming away on the old blood sausage, I had decided to treat her to that holy grail of female sensual pleasure, an anal orgasm.

"Take that Greer woman for instance," I carried on referring to my little teenage buggeree's namesake. "I mean that ugly old cow, she's just plain and simply a nasty, bossy, fucking cunt. Nothing else. All that theorising and shit is just there to somehow back up, justify and ultimately camouflage her deeply unpleasant personality."

Some women are just born that way, miserable, selfish, determined to have their own way no matter what, all throughout their entire bitter and miserable lives.

Zodiac Mindwarp

"I got a mean machine baby
It's an obscene limousine
I feel OK when I gun my Chevrolet
I wanna blow the circuits on your
love machine
Cos I'm a hi-tech cupid with an M-16
Storm the gates of Heaven
On wheels made in Hell"

*take a trip
behind my zip*

MARK MANNING

Now a bitch like that, any decent bloke's going to avoid like the fucking plague.

It stands to reason.

And that's the real reason why these mentaloid feminist idiots hate men. Because they've never had a real one.

I mean what healthy, normal, sane bloke wants to fuck a grumpy old bag like her and then receive some stupid fucking lecture about his sexual fanny-licking technique afterwards.

You know what I'm saying?

Fuck that for a game of soldiers!

My little buggery bird was squealing like a stuck pig, wriggling away on the very cusp of the ultimate female sexual bumhole orgasm.

"Of course," I continued grandly, still thrusting expertly away. "There is a certain type of man that likes all this angry fucked-up woman shit – if you can call them men that is – bend-over boyfriends is what I call them. Pussy-whipped fuckers who do exactly as their mouthy, *Cosmopolitan*-reading bitch tells them. Sly bastards who pretend to agree with all their girlfriends' mentally ill, modern feministic theories whilst secretly indulging themselves in some covert SM fantasy about Ms Susan Faluhdi or one of the other frigid horsehair-minge bitches cracking a whip across their submissive white arses."

I snapped off a great oyster of bollock jam up little Germaine's arse and the sweet deluded young thing juddered to the stars, experiencing wave after wave of deeply erotic sensations as she exploded internally from her very first anal orgasm.

"Oh my God, you're so right master!!" she screamed, blorping her arse off of my shiny purple reptile and collapsing into a sated puddle on the beer-soaked carpet.

"Yes, yes, we've all been such naïve fools," echoed one of her feminist sisters as she too juddered to a buggery orgasm, old Tex bucking away on her shitlocker like there was no tomorrow.

Boss feminist groaned and was silent for once in her life.

The poor bitch had been so overcome by the gibbering intensity of her sodomistic orgasms that she had died.

Rock and roll baby.

It's not all bad.

JACK DANIELS RASTA

It was Charlie Bumfucker, our A&R man's idea.

And it was fucking crap even by his standards.

Get Lee Scratch Perry to remix "Back Street Education", our second single for Cosmosodomistic Records.

Lee Scratch fucking Perry. I mean, like why?

It wasn't as if we were a bunch of West London wannabe fucking spades or anything, we weren't the Clash or John fucking Lydon.

Not that I've got anything against black people, I just think that their music is shit and that their clothes are too big.

I mean I can't stand fucking reggae, dub, whatever that dope-smoking mega-reverb bollocks is called.

It just reminds me of whores, pimps, political lesbos, fresh criminals just out of jail, drug dealers, cheap muggers, art students and transvestites.

Actually it reminds me of The International club in Bradford.

A real sleazehole dive of a place that existed on that scabrous city's notorious Lumb Lane in the seventies.

Lumb Lane was where the Yorkshire Ripper collared most of his sluts.

The place has changed a lot these days, almost looks respectable, new council estates, sandstone, community renewal, all that bollocks.

But back in the mid-seventies Lumb Lane was the nearest the North of England ever got to the fabled arse-ripping biblical wickedness of Sodom and Gommorah.

The place was virtually a no-go zone for cops, like Northern Ireland but without the politics.

Whatever evil monkey pulled your chain you could buy it up there on the Northern slopes of the Colne Valley.

Smack, buggery, bondage, curry.

All freely available at the most competitive rates around.

And all of this whore-ripping, dope-smoking, homosexual, paedophiliac, maniac monstering with mongols-on-day-release-from-children's-homes was conducted to a fuck awful soundtrack of psychedelic, spliffed out, dub reggae, arseshit, chinka chinka, illegal, fucking junglemusic music.

Well in my head it was.

Which is why I hated reggae.

MARK MANNING

It just reminded me of sexual perversion and crime.

But what the fuck, I was just the artist.

If Charlie boy wanted to flex creative and throw more dollars down the record company fucking toilet who was I to object.

So me Cobalt, Slam and the Gimp turned up all sullen at Matrix studios to meet some black lunatic who was being paid cash to remix and ruin our latest rocking masterpiece.

I liked the cat instantly.

He was totally insane.

A short guy with grey hair, no dreads, mirrors sellotaped to his commando boots, fucking full-on loony, he gripped my hand and stared meaningfully into my eye.

I smiled, eyes twinkling and everything, I think he liked me, he bent double and started doing one of those Jamaican donkey-type laughs, hee hawing and slapping his knee and shit. Then as fast as a weasel escaping from some West Indian hurricane his mood switched and he got all serious.

Gazing off into some horizon only the dubmaster genius himself had access to, he proclaimed grandly: "Rock and roll, the magic scroll." And told me to follow him into the toilet.

There were microphones wired up to the bog and the sink and stuff. Scratch flushed the toilet and said "Water," and looked at me as though he had just revealed some great arcane secret.

"Yeah man, water," I said, a little confused. "Groovy."

I followed him into the mixing room, he'd been busy, the whole place was decked out in fairy lights, joss sticks, candles, crucifixes, weird broken mirrors hanging from the light fittings. A massive spliff, really fucking massive, about a foot long, smouldered in the ash tray. Empty bottles of peach brandy littered the floor, he wiped the neck of his current half-destroyed one and offered me a swig. The cat was wasted.

He jabbered something in drunken Jamaican patois at the engineer who dutifully played back the unholy mess he'd made of our track.

It just sounded as if he'd taken everything out of the mix except for the bass and drums and put shit loads of echo on it.

What the fuck did I care, that peach brandy tasted pretty good.

I took a hit on the biggest spliff in the world and went into the TV lounge.

Fuck it I thought, coasting on the madman's sensi, "Gimpo, go and get a

couple of bottles of Jack, I think it's going to be a long session."

I mean really there was no reason we should have been there at all, remixes are usually conducted in some obscure studio with some breadhead fucking around with expensive effects racks and other studio horseshit, pissing around with another's magic and picking up a fat check from the idiots who run record companies at the end of it.

But we were young rocking spunkers and the inevitable cynicism that comes with any job that one is effortlessley good at hadn't evolved yet.

We still thought that our music was important.

So it was equally important that we sat around the studio getting shit-faced, arguing with each other and listening to the progressive stages of fucked-upness Scratch was making of our recording.

I mean we didn't care, there was no way even the most cloth-eared fucking arsehole at Cosmosodom was going to put out this load of reverbed, spliffed-out drunken bollocks that the mad reggae meister was cooking up in his little peach brandy shabeen. Even *they* weren't that fucking stupid.

"What the fuck is he doing in there?" said Slam, we'd finished the first bottle of Jack and had sent Gimpo out to buy three more before the offy closed. "Is that us?"

The music spiralling out of the mixing room was starting to defy description, I mean there's dub and there's like mental fucking illness.

This shit didn't even sound like it was recorded on earth.

Some black guy wandered into the studio, I'd met him a few times before.

Typical rasta, lived completely outside of reality, I didn't know what the fuck he was talking about half the time.

He was pleasant enough though, looked a bit like a very young Bob Marley but like I say, I just didn't know what the fuck he was on about most of the time.

He would be talking sort of normally in English and stuff and then he would start grandly pontificating about I and I and all kinds of other weird black crap, usually Jah whoever the fuck he was, Babylon and bamba claats, all delivered at top volume in this weird, theatrical, bogus West Indian accent.

I guess it must be all the dope they smoke or something.

The kid knew the studio manager, who would let him use the studio down time to record his meandering marijuana dub masterpieces and he'd dropped by to find out when he could complete his latest dub epic.

MARK MANNING

The little rastaboy nearly shit a kitten when he found out that Lee Scratch Perry, *the* Lee Scratch Perry was in the mixing room working on one of our tracks.

"You've got Scratch remixing one of your tracks?" he said in English, absolutely incredulous that the king of drug music had deigned to work with a bunch of white arseholes like us.

I mean the twenty-five grand in cash probably had a lot to do with it, but poor people don't understand this, especially poor musicians who are usually not very intelligent, they think that everyone is as artistically pure as themselves and that all art is done for art's sake.

That state of affairs unfortunately, in all strands of the arts only ever happens at the beginning; as soon as the Dollar God rears its ugly, penis-breath head, forget it, we're into repetition mode.

"Yeah man, he's in there now fucking up our latest single," I said, a little confused by the kid's deep reverence.

I mean I just thought he was some Jamaican mentaloid, I didn't realise he was the king of spliff-rock dubmaster far-out reggae geniusness.

"I've got to meet him, can I go in?" said fanboy.

"Yeah man just go in, he's not the queen or anything," I answered bemused.

At this point King Scratch stumbled red-eyed out of the studio, and seemed a little surprised at seeing a fellow black person in whitey's den.

He started doing a little jig and talking in that weird patois with all the I and I's and Rastafari shit.

I don't know what he had said, but little Timmy Marley had got the hump bigtime. "What feh is you doing with dem white bwoys!" said Tiny Bob, obviously pissed off.

"Me doing the back street heducation!" said Scratch, all indignant. "It am de big bwoy's music," he answered giving junior rasta the evil eye.

"Don't feh to fuck with me bossman, Rastafari," said junior, pulling off his hat and shaking his dreads like a headful of snakes.

Scratch threw his beany hat to the floor and rubbed his grey number one crop vigorously. "This am de best hair!" he shouted, and jack-knifed into hysterical knee-slapping Jamaican donkey laughs again.

The poor kid obviously understood what all this black shit was all about, kicked a hole in the wall and stomped out of the studio, dissed, or whatever it is they call it.

Scratch laughed out loud and returned to the mixing suite shouting out something about a babystar.

Like I say, I didn't have a clue what these mad black fellows were on about. We just got back into the Jack and started making fun of Gimpo.

It seemed like Scratch had run out of his peach brandy. The Jamaican dubmaster shaman stumbled out of the mixing suite.

"What am dat white bwoy shit?" he said pointing at the bottle of Jack Daniels sat there all dangerous on our table.

"Erm, it's American whiskey," said Slam. "It makes you go mental and get all dangerous," he added. "Do you want some?"

"Gimme dat shit," said Scratch teetering wildly.

Well it kicked off then. And I guess we kind of bonded.

We all piled into the studio, drinking and smoking Scratch's homicidal ganga, pushing buttons and faders till all the red danger lights looked as if they were about to explode. The engineer looked terrified.

And then Gimpo got his fireworks out. I don't know what it is about Gimpo, he seems to carry fireworks around with him the same way that other people carry fags or house keys. The dub monstrosity of "Back Seat Education" sounded fucking great with bangers, catherine wheels, jumping crackers, airbombs and rockets going off though. Scratch was in hysterics rolling around the floor. I couldn't believe he had never drunk Jack Daniels before. We fucked around in that small studio beneath Coptic Street till about eight the next morning. As usual the fire brigade turned up several times and the studio bill was somewhere in the stratosphere.

The track?

Don't ever let Jack Daniels remix anything.

Ever.

WORLD'S LONGEST WANK

"What the fucking hell was that?" said Cobalt, wiping off a humongous bollock oyster of cock snot from the back of his funky mohican hairstyle. "You dirty fucking bastard!" he added, realising what revolting body fluid had just splattered the back of his head.

"Fuck, shit, I'm sorry Cobalt," laughed Slam, his new girlfriend snickering wickedly beside him.

We were sat in a cramped mini-bus, me and Cobalt in the middle seats, Slam and his little cock-frigger on the back ones.

We were nearly in Cannes in the South of France, Slam had been getting tossed off for the entire length of the country, right from Calais where we left the ferry to just outside the Riviera town where we were about to appear on some dumb TV show.

Seven solid hours of being wanked off.

Amazing.

I'm surprised that the poor girl's arm hadn't dropped off.

It had been a few weeks after the bucket of piss incident and Slam had finally realised that his sexual trespasses were never to be forgiven.

The Mrs had kicked him out for good and he could fucking go ahead and kill himself for all she cared. If he ever came round again next time it would be a bucket of shit on his cheating, philandering, good-looking head.

Back off buster, fuck off, drop dead, the works.

So after crying for about three minutes Slam had decided, quite wisely, to avail himself of a few of the pneumatic fleshpots that perpetually lurked around the trough of rocking excess that we were all currently gorging ourselves at.

It hadn't taken him long to realise that the sexually alluring bogus glamour of our new rock stars on the block status wouldn't last forever and that he had better get in there fast and pork whatever was available.

Except unfortunately, old Slammy wasn't that good at it really, boning sluts that is.

If the truth be known poor old Slam was just too much of a decent fellow.

He lacked the obsidian callousness of Cobalt and myself.

The fucking idiot even talked politely in hotel lobbys and breakfast rooms to some of his venereal conquests.

The sentimental idiot actually treated some of these fanny-farting, spunk-belching, penis-breath slatterns as if they were real, live human beings.

Big mistake.

Successful slag-shagging takes a heart that is as hard and insensitive as your heartless slag-shagging dick.

I mean the fucking imbecile had actually been fucking some of these vile cabbage-bucket bitches in the flapping, distended, tangle of suppurating flesh that was their ugly vaginas.

Something that was absolutely and totally unthinkable for the Stargazer and myself. We were both solidly committed arsehole men.

"What!?" said Cobalt, dumbstruck when he found out that his percussive friend had been sticking his cock in that unnatural groupie orifice, the front bottom. "You shagged her in her gash!" he continued, horrified. "What on earth made you do that? For fuck's sake you do realise that there is a slight possibility that the bitch might have actually enjoyed it!"

Poor Slam looked confused. "Well erm, yeah, isn't that kind of like the point Cobalt?" he offered, looking extremely perplexed.

"With a normal girl, yeah, maybe," elucidated the enlightened guitarist to his slightly dim pal, "But not with a road hog you fucking idiot, Jesus Christ man they might come back for more!"

"Fucking hell. I never thought of that," said Slam wising up instantly. "But I fucked her really badly though, she didn't come or anything," he added, remembering the feminists and trying to cover over his incredible *faux pas*.

"It's best not to take any chances at all Slam," I chipped in, adding my two penneth to Slam's crash course in how to deal with the syphilitic heaps that were groupies. "And don't use any lubrication either, not even spit, bang them ultra fast in the arse and unload the nad jam as quickly as possible. Think of yourself as a WW2 bomber pilot who has to dump his bombload as soon as he can and then head straight back to Blighty," I continued with my sage counsel.

"Why do I have to do it so fast?" questioned the naïve sticksman.

"Fucking hell Slam, are you totally fucking stupid?" said Cobalt, exasperated by Slams naïveté. "For fuck's sake man, believe it or not there are actually one or two mentally ill bitches out there that actually *like* having their bumholes destroyed!"

"Get the fuck out of here!" said Slam. "A piledriver up the shitter, they like it? God almighty, are you fucking serious, what, they want to wear fucking colostomy bags for the rest of their lives or something? What's fucking wrong with them?"

"I wouldn't worry too much though," I said seriously. "I mean if I ever come across a bird with a Boy George-type ringpiece I just throw her out of the window. Or give her to Gimpo." Trying to put our friend at ease, but the poor chap was starting to look decidedly perturbed.

"So remember Slam, arse only, and make it snappy. I don't even shag my girlfriend in the cunt any more," said Cobalt. "Just to keep her in line mind. The last thing you want to do is give a woman sexual pleasure, they just lose all respect for you, the next thing you know you're having to cook your own food," added the world-wise cocksman.

"And wash your own clothes," I added, gilding the lily somewhat.

"God you're fucking right," said Slam. "Arse only, arse only," he muttered in a profane pervert mantra, wandering off behind his drumkit.

Of course the fucking chump took absolutely no fucking notice of we wise arsemasters' advice, and within one week found himself in love with one of the biggest cabbage slingers in New York City.

I mean don't get me wrong.

Ramona was no common or garden NY salami jockey.

The bitch was premier, grade A, ball-draining, super-gash.

Big Angelina Jolie bell-end snarfing mouth on her, tits like a couple of babies wrestling in a pillowcase and an arse like Michelangelo's David.

No spunk-swallowing, Staines, Barnsley, JB's in Dudley bicycle-type bird here.

She was full-on, rock star cock only, proper fully paid up, union member, professional big time cock-sucking super-groupie.

One up from a common whore.

But still a whore.

The payments were just more tricky to trace, that's all.

Airfares, free drugs, hotels, all that crap.

I mean don't get me wrong, these girls serve a purpose, save many a flimsy entertainment industry marriage.

These bitches, the smart ones, know their place.

They don't call you at home for instance.

Hearts as hard as any hard rocker.

But old Slammy didn't quite understand any of this.

Him being a decent fellow and all.

He thought she was a nice girl that loved him.

Well, he *was* a drummer.

And we don't really need any light bulb jokes about that profession do we?

Of course the Slamster eventually wised up when he kind of realised that everybody in the rocking world that we came across all seemed to hesitantly sort of know his new girlfriend.

If you know what I mean.

"Oh yeah, Ramona, Tokyo, New York, Los Angeles, Paris," kind of thing.

So the drummer dumped the slut and promptly fell in love with a new chick called Heidi in LA.

Heidi Sausage.

As she was known by The Cure's charming road crew.

I mean even by Slam's standards this one really took the jizz-soaked biscuit.

We were sitting in a Dennys burger joint on some lost highway in the middle of Mid West nowhere purgatory America.

"What the fuck?" said Cobalt, coughing up his coffee.

"What?" said Slam, surprised.

"You've got like, little bugs crawling in your moustache," replied guitar boy, fingering Slam's facial hair like a monkey grooming a fellow simian.

"Slam, you cunt," he continued, starting to laugh. "You've got fucking crabs in your beard!"

Heidi Sausage.

I rest my case.

ACCIDENTAL HOMO

We all know this one.

Even women.

That transitional period between sleep and awakening.

When for some bizarre reason we believe that we are loved.

And we have to genitally react.

Probing and fudging.

The only thing was though.

We had a sleepwalker in our midst.

Not only that.

It was Gimpo.

Sexually insane bone-on man.

The horror, the horror.

Oh creepiness, let me tell you brother.

The most horrible thing that ever happened to me in my life.

When Gimpo tried to bum me.

It was the Slammer that had paved the way for this dreadful experience.

We were in some bomb-forgotten shitehole in Germany.

A big festival-type thing.

Loads of teenagers in a field pissing in plastic bottles and shedding major deutschmarks to groove on the musical expressions of a bunch of deeply fucked-up sad bad men.

Guns and Mongols were the big draw.

A bunch of LA sociopaths who had got lucky somewhere down the dollar machine. Slam was good buddies with the rhythm section.

I couldn't be arsed with all that socialising crap.

I was on a mission.

As all lead singers are.

But Slammy he was courting these whiskey-stinking reprobates.

Maybe when we imploded he could get a sticks job with these lowlife super losers.

So he's hanging out with Guff, the bass player, rhythm section thing.

But to cut to the point.

Slammy and the Gimp, who was in tow, get put up in the super monster hotel.

Except that they're short of a bed – well no problem, kip up together.

Whoah, sunshine.

The morning poking starts.

"What, like he had a lobb-on and everything?"

"Yeah man, motherfucker is probing away behind me."

"Get the fuck out of here," said Cobalt, extremely disturbed.

We had a closet fudgepacker amongst us.

This was worse than fucking *Alien*.

"He was asleep though," said Slam, defending our demented friend.

"Oh my god. A somnambulist bummer, maybe we should kill him," I said equally frightened.

So six months later I'm like dragged from sleep in the danger of my own bed.

And there looming above me, with a hard-on, is the sleepwalking Gimp.

I think I've said enough.

Just calling up the memory is making my arse shiver.

And no, he didn't.

I decked the fucker.

NO TENNANTS SUPER ON THE RIDER AGAIN.
NEVER, EVER.

Read the minutes of our band meeting.

How the fucking hell we thought we could get away with that one is anybody's guess.

Tennants Super on the rider?

Twelve fucking cans each every night for three months?

Tennants Super for anyone not in the know is that foul-tasting, treacly rocket fuel that tramps drink.

We loved it.

The mother of my son used to work in advertising and was once commissioned to do some work for the Tennants Brewery organization. She was being consulted advertising-wise by the company about some other, more socially acceptable drink that the mighty Scottish brewery produced, and in passing she mentioned this potent particular brew.

She was interested as to how the people who made the stuff viewed their product, seeing as how it was almost killing the father of her son and ruining her relationship with him beyond all repair.

The arrogant Scot thought that she was asking as to why the purple-tinned monstrosity was never advertised, well she *was* an advertising consultant. Jock the poisoner simply replied "Street drinkers and Afro-Caribbeans." As if this was enough.

My ex didn't pursue it and took an instant dislike to the man as most people instinctively do when in the company of drugs and arms dealers.

People that profit on other people's misery that is.

So when and where did my love affair begin with this purple poison first begin?

I was first made aware of it back in the early eighties.

My artschool friend Val Denham and his young wife Elita had found themselves a cosy flat in Streatham, my first wife Christine was best friends with Elita and I was close with Val so we often visited.

Val produced a can of this innocuous-looking stuff from the fridge and asked if I wanted to try it, warning me that it was extremely strong and somewhat of an acquired taste.

Of course I didn't believe him at the time, being a young and inexperienced pisshead. People were always saying such and such a drink was particularly potent. Usually as an excuse for some or other piece of extraordinarily anti-social behaviour. I think this must have been the time before it was legally compulsory to put the alcohol content on the label of all alcoholic beverages, as one never knew how strong anything was and it was all a bit of pot luck. Of course these days I can pretty much guess to within one percent what the strength of any drink is, just by taste.

I'm an extremely knowledgeable and experienced shitface artist.

But back then I just thought he was talking bollocks. "No seriously Mark, it's not like other drinks," said Val, pouring me a glass.

"Yeah, yeah," I replied, pulling a face like lemons and sour onions, the stuff tasted like tramp's vomit.

"Fucking Elita drinks it all the time, she goes mental," he added. "Martin was over the other night and Elita got pissed on the stuff, she was jumping around on the settee rubbing her fanny with a vibrator, saying come on Martin do you fuckin' want some. I mean Elita? She's just not like that."

Needless to say I couldn't drink more than a mouthful so it took a few years before I realised that Val was absolutely right and that Tennants Super was an extremely dangerous drink indeed.

Kind of like a low-rent cousin of absinthe.

But to get back to the Tennants Superman tour.

It seemed like the band had gone from playing humongodromes to playing the Arse and Racket in Chingford overnight. It had actually taken a good couple of years but all of us were so fucking blasted pretty much all of the time that none of us even noticed. So obviously when I did realise that my fortunes were pretty much waning megaforce five rapido, I turned to my liquid ego-soother in even greater quantities and, as is inevitable I ended up drinking with bums.

On the street.

In Camden.

On that little fucking wall outside the tube station.

Tennants.

It was only when a fan recognised me and took me into a pub to try and talk some sense into me that I thought maybe I might have had a problem.

As it was I got even more pissed, kicked the landlord's dog and got chased out of the joint by some cunt threatening to brain me with a piece of four by two.

I mention this as apropos of nothing, as seems appropriate when discussing the purple tin, since everything under the influence of that fucking stuff is apropos of nothing.

Which kind of brings me back to the point.

Which I've forgotten.

So fuck off.

See what I mean?

Even talking about the Devil's favourite tipple gets me all confused, you ramble, talk a load of bollocks up one tree then go and piss on another one. A whole three-month tour of that shit we had.

When writing this book I would often meet up with Cobalt and Bill, Evil Bastard and all the other fuckers involved in this mighty disarraying of the senses. Try to pick their brains, remember some of the details so I could warn you of the dangers of seizing that fucking day that any sensible person would leave well alone – and I am invariably met with a brick wall of no memory at all.

That's what alcohol at arse-shivering levels of insanity does.

It removes all responsibility.

Lets you be yourself.

No wonder we all love it so much.

Here's to Bacchus and Poussin's immaculate rendering of him.

The David Weill room in the National Gallery, check it out.

We have a pedigree.

POTHEAD WANKER
DRAMATIS PERSONAE #2: SUZY X

It was just like an MTV video.

Cobalt was sailing through the air in slow motion, his guitar twisting poetic behind him.

Then crunch.

I came out of the blackout covered in blood and broken glass.

Cobalt's big fat arse was crushing my head through the side window of the van and I could smell petrol.

Somewhere Robbie was squawking at the top of his voice. "Don't panic! Don't panic!" And panicking like fuck.

We'd just skidded off the side of a French Alp.

I'd been in a couple of crashes before, so unlike the earlier experiences I knew what had happened as soon as I heard that fuck-awful crump of buckling metal and breaking glass.

I'd never seen the slow motion shit before though.

Apparently it's a common experience in near death experiences.

The adrenaline supposedly slows down your perception of time so as to allow a few extra seconds so that you can biologically get out of the way of grizzly bears and prehistoric monsters, dodge bullets in war, that kind of thing.

Some sort of atavistic, biological, survival thing that scientists invented.

Well, whatever, the adrenaline, slow motion, biological, atavistic Sam Peckinpah shit didn't help me get out of the way of Cobalt's arse. Blam! the sexy fretboard fatboy's giant khyber crunched my head straight through the van's side window and into the snow, almost breaking my cheekbone and bending my gigs way into geekoid mode.

It was another one of those weird Euro tours.

The places where bands go to die when nobody loves them any more.

If no-one wants you in England, your notoriety is good for at least five or so more years in obscure French, German and Scandinavian versions of Barnsley and Scunthorpe.

So there we were, riding around the rock graveyard in some smoky shitty little transit thing with a hole in the floor where all the diesel fumes came through, making us cough. Joe was at the wheel.

We were en route from Le Barnslee to Scunthorpio right on top of the French

MARK MANNING

Italian Alps. "Brace yourselves lads!" said Joe in slow motion, looking over his shoulder.

I remember seeing the blizzard outside the window, thinking how pretty it looked as the van slid slowly at a weird angle along the icy road, like one of those things that you shake with a cute Christmas thing in it.

We rolled down the side of the elevated road, turning five or six times, the van crunched up like a crisp bag. Joe and Suzy were thrown through the windscreen, even more like a video, as we waltzed down the mountain.

Groovy.

I somehow managed to shove Cobalt's arse off my head and check to see if my bollocks were still there.

They were.

It was just another crash.

I didn't give a fuck about feet, legs, arms etc. As long as I had my bollocks, my hands and my eyes everything was alright.

We were all pretty much OK, lots of blood and lacerations, bruises and stuff, I think Joe cracked a couple of ribs – but at least we weren't dead. Somehow we managed to crawl back up to the side of the road.

We stood there for half an hour, in a fucking blizzard, freezing and bleeding. Not one of those French, Italian cunts stopped to offer any help.

I guess we did look pretty scary though.

Shivering, bloody in our stinking denim and grubby T-shirts with "fuck off" written across them.

Zombie drug-eating Apocalypse hitch hikers from Hell.

"Don't stop Marie Clare! Don't stop!" screams Pierre Fellatio in a passing Citroen to his pretty young wife. "Don't stop for those zombie drug-eating Apocalypse hitch hikers from English Hell!"

Obviously some righteous citizen must have called the cops on their cellular, because just as hypothermia and delirium tremens were kicking in, along sirened les snowboy emergency rozzeurs.

Rescued.

We were patched up and dumped in some strange Catholic hotel.

It was the kind of place that touring bands never usually find themselves staying at. Tours are arranged and things are all organized so that shit runs relatively smoothly, the hotels are usually au fait with the incontinent drug-abusing habits and alcohol-crippled ways of we high decibel pariahs.

But this place. They had French squaddies staying there. This was not a regular rock and roll hotel. The manageress made us all go to bed at eleven o' fucking clock.

The next day we found a brand new bus waiting outside for us.

Somehow we were insured. Why, how or who arranged this I have no idea but the bus was just peachy. It wasn't a regular tour bus with bunks and videos and shit, it was more of a transport type thing, with loads of seats. A kind of French national express type vibe. After the transit death van with the diesel fumes and no heating this ordinary single decker felt like fucking Concorde.

We set off for Switzerland, happy as shit. All of us except for old laughing boy Suzy that is, Suzy X; grumpiest spliff-smoking occult bass player in the world.

Suzy was being even slower and mongoloid than ever, he'd bought himself a huge piece of stinky black hash from the soldiers and was trying to smoke it all before we got to the Swiss border.

One of the many rock rules of the road, like not shitting in the chemical shitter and stuff, is that no drugs are to be taken across borders. This is an entirely practical arrangement because buses and equipment can be impounded by zealous customs officials, therefore scuppering highly expensive tours, wages for crews, promotors' fees, all that crap.

Besides, drugs aren't exactly difficult to find in Europe, especially if you're a member of a lowlife scumbag itinerant rock band.

Pothead Suzy was always smuggling pieces of hash all over the place, the fucking idiot, but not today. Sick of being bollocked by Cobalt for his rock rule-breaking, the intelligent bass player had decided that rather than waste his precious dope he would eat the fucking lot of it.

My God, fucking horrible.

We were approaching the Swiss border when Cobalt decided to go and check that our forgetful bass player wasn't running the risk of blowing out a fifty grand tour for a twenty quid deal of dope. The red-eyed bass bumbler had been sat in a huge cloud of evil-smelling smoke all in his own right at the back of the bus for ages.

We hadn't heard a peep out of the stoned drug baboon for hours, we assumed he was doing some astral travelling or some other arse-weird marijuana occult bollocks.

MARK MANNING

"Oh my fucking God!" said Cobalt before collapsing in hysterical laughter.

"Z, Robbie come and look at this!" Cobalt was laughing so loud I thought he was going to shit himself. We ran to the back of the bus – what a sight.

Comatose Suzy doped out of his brains had decided to have himself a sneaky little drug tug. Pants around his ankles, he held his flaccid white, dead slug cock in one hand and a shitty black and white porno mag in the other. A string of clear cock snot stretched from his circumsised bell-end to his skinny inner thigh. T-shirt covered in ball gravy. He had his head resting mongishly on his shoulder and his glasses had slipped to the end of his nose, his tongue was lolling out of his slack jaw, drool dripping off his chin.

What a fucking sight.

He looked like some kind of Downs Syndrome Benny Hill Fred Scuttle wank monster. "The fucking chosen people or what?" laughed Robbie, referring to Suzy's Jewish parentage. "What's he been tugging over, pass it here," he added.

We checked out the masturbating Hebrew's tug of choice.

"Oh fucking hell, not another one, are you all fucking shit-stabbers in this fucking band, or what!" said drumming boy, which was rich coming from Mr bumhole-licking-through-the-knickers himself, Robbie Vomm.

Suzy's delightful little magazine was called *Arse Maidens Of Agony* and contained nothing but extreme close-up, black and white pictures of German women's bumholes being tortured with pins, clamps, wires, ferrets and stuff. Cobalt took a photograph of wanker Samuel and the next day sent it to Suzy's girlfriend, who finished with him immediately.

Served him right, fucking tugger.

THE WORST THING THAT COULD HAPPEN TO ANYONE IN THE WORLD, EVER

Gimpo shags your bird.

Not only that, he moves in with her.

And they have a kid together.

I'd kill myself.

But Suzy was probably so stoned he more than likely didn't even notice.

Why, if you're a fucking idiot, you may ask, is the idea of Gimpo as opposed to anyone else shagging your wife such a terrible thought.

Listen, we all know the Gimp, all know of his vile sexual ways, have seen him in action, buggering Rohypnol'd groupies whilst watching porn vids, shitting.

He would do it right there in front of us, in the fucking hotel room.

We would be all sat around drinking petrol and snorting heroin and monsterboy would be over in some corner bumming the shite out of his latest victim, fucking slippery turds all over the fucking place.

It wasn't nice.

Poor Suzy he gets back from his dope dealer with his regular week's supply of half a pound of paki black.

The slack fucker rolls a fat one, and another, and another, as druggies do.

Three days later he realises that the woman he's been living with for the past three years isn't around.

Probably because there's no bog roll or some other domestic crap that always seems to fall to a woman to look after, men aren't quite as fussy about what they wipe their arses on, old newspapers, soap wrappers, even cigarette coupons, who gives a shit.

So Suzy X who smokes dope for England is having a big stoned dump and having to wipe his arse on yesterday's *Guardian* when he slowly realises that he hasn't seen his partner for three days.

The bumbling pothead, spliff as ever in hand wanders around the small flat, four hours later he finds the letter, right under his nose on top of his beloved sampler.

"Dear Suzy," it begins. "I am leaving you.

You are a lazy, useless, selfish bastard. You spend all of my hard-earned

MARK MANNING

money on drugs and are always so stoned you can't even be arsed to knob me any more.

Fuck off I hate you.

I'm moving in with Gimpo and I am going to suck his cock forever and have a baby with him.

Don't try to get in touch with me, if you do Gimpo will smash your head in.

Piss off, get stuffed,

Love Emma."

You had to feel sorry for him.

The poor cunt.

I mean, Gimpo.

How many stories had he had to sit around listening to on those long rolling barnyard treks across arctic tundras.

Those grisly ferries across English channels, Norwegian fjörds and other stretches of black water.

The Gimp like some feral, wanking, Jizz Shaman would be sat around an imaginary camp fire, can of beer and spliff in either hand, regaling us with all the anal horror of his shite-besmirched, grotesque, transgressive sexual crimes.

The Gimp, who seriously believes that rape should be made legal.

"I got her back to my place right, stuck my hands down the front of her knickers, she was fucking soaking, dripping she was, smelled like fucking Grimsby. I got down on my knees, had her fucking pissflaps round my fucking ears. Moaning like I was fucking murdering her. When you get them that fucking juiced up right –" Gimpo uses the word right and the word fucking like punctuation, commas and full fucking stops, right. "– they don't know what the fuck's going on, flip 'em over on their belly and stab it up the shitter, fucking lovely, you know what I mean? right. Fucking slag."

I mean there's nothing unusual about all of this.

Most women soak up like the North Sea when their boilers have been stoked long and hard enough, it's just that mostly we men don't discuss our gruesome fannybatter peregrinations with our womenfolk amongst other sleazebags.

Not if we love them, care about them, are terrified of them, that kind of thing, we don't.

But the Gimp he didn't give a fuck, every sordid detail would be regaled in

the most sordid language I think only armed forces trained bullet morons are capable of. "This little four-eyed cunt right, in the Falklands right.

Only fucking bird on the fucking island right.

Worked in the fish and fucking chip shop. I think she was a fucking mongofuckingloid or something, looked like a big fat fucking pixie.

Well there was no other fucking fanny on the fucking place so one night right, we all got our fish and fucking chips right and started messing around with her, joking and fucking around and all that bollocks, fucking dozy spaz cunt, we gave her a right fucking seeing to, you know what I mean, fucking mong bitch fucking loved it she fucking did, spunk all over the fucking place, in her fucking hair, fucking everywhere man. I tell you man them fucking mongy birds, ugly fucking cunts but they can't half fucking go. You know what I fucking mean? Fuck, fuck."

I mean Suzy, drugged into some supernatural state of occult consciousness had to listen to this bollocks night after night. "So I says are you into shitting? Fucking bitch was so fucking drunk she didn't know what the fuck I was fucking on about. Thought I was asking if she wanted to go to fucking toilet. I fucking poured more booze in her right, and then shat on her fucking face, rubbed it in and then gave her arse a right fucking seeing-to, threw her out on the fucking street at four in the fucking morning, fucking slag, watched her hobble down the street, looking for a fucking cab, from the fucking hotel window."

The thing is, Suzy only ever heard about these things.

I fucking fucking witnessed fucking them on more than one fucking fucking occasion.

I mean I shared a flat with the monster for nearly ten years.

The horror that I heard spiralling out of the Gimp's room in the small hours defies description.

I would wake up needing a piss and stumble to the bathroom.

There, chained to the radiator, quivering in fear, eyes wide open, gagged, covered in excrement would be another of the monster's conquests.

I mean, it started getting normal to me.

"Excuse me love I just need to take a piss," I would say pushing the drugged girl out of the way, wondering where on earth the Gimp found these degenerates.

What that says about me, God only knows.

MARK MANNING

I mean, if I'm really honest the only thing that really bothered me was the smell.

So yeah man, the worst thing that could ever happen to anyone in the world ever.

Ever, ever, ever.

Gimpo nicks your bird.

Good God.

Right.

Fucking.

You know what I mean?

Suzy X.

Ha ha ha.

It couldn't have happened to a nicer drug addict.

FASHION WANKERS

Of course it was never really going to catch on.

Our unique fashion statement that no-one apart from thirteen-year-old girls ever noticed that is.

Spunk stains up the front of our T-shirts.

As a band we were probably the most sexually insane eight-legged thing that ever prowled the face of God's green earth.

If we weren't fucking, fighting or drinking we were probably wanking.

Every city in Europe, the first thing we would do would be to find the nearest death shop. Those weird psycho shacks that sell martial arts equipment.

After we'd bought a rake of knives, nunchackas, spears, tommy guns and incendiary bombs, we would always then check out the nearest wanking emporium.

I love how they call them sex shops, as that is exactly what they are not.

I mean you can't buy sex in them, the only things they sell are magazines, videos and ugly pink plastic things.

Scary veiny knobs and horsehair rubber fannies made in China to help you along with the wanking.

Somehow I guess though, Wanking Shop doesn't have the same allure.

At least if it's called a sex shop you can kind of pretend that you're having some kind of sex.

If you're a lonely tugger who hasn't had a girlfriend for fifteen years I mean.

But that's what they are though.

Shops staffed by wankers, owned by wankers, catering for wankers.

It's terrible I know but it's true.

I mean we didn't give a fuck.

We were full-on wankers, were even proud of it in a strange kind of way.

I mean, "I'd rather have a fucking wank than fuck you, you fucking bitch," how cool is that.

Some skank is all over you wanting you to fall in love with her so that she can make your life miserable and spend all your easy-earned money. And you tell her straight. That you'd rather fuck your fist than get involved with a money-siphoning, three-holed piece of spunk cabbage, cock-sucking, dogshit like her.

Anyway that's my justifications for being a tosser out of the way, let's get

MARK MANNING

back to my fashion article.

Us four wankers are sat around in some French hotel. Me, the Stargazer, Kid Chaos and Monsieur Thunderhide watching ourselves being interviewed on some teatime light-hearted after the main national news TV show type thing.

We're all talking crap and flirting mildly with the flirty French bimbo who is employed specifically to flirt with drunken rock idiots.

"Fucking hell Z," said Kid Chaos eating a sardine and whipped cream baguette. I know, fucking horrible. "Look at your T-shirt!"

"What?" I replied, looking at my AC/DC T-shirt on the TV.

"You can see all the spunk up the front of it, where you've been wanking," he said starting to laugh.

"Fucking hell, he's right and all," said Cobalt, coughing up his pint of Jack and coke.

And he was.

There on French national TV I'm sat talking a load of crap with some French TV actress slut with a big fucking shiny spunk slug trail up the front of my black T-shirt.

I must admit it did give me a slight thrill. Sitting there with my sperm stains in front of a French girl who hadn't even been properly introduced to me. It was kind of like having my cock out or something, and she did have nice tights on, those shiny ones.

Well it kind of caught on with the rest of us.

Wandering around everywhere with massive spunk stains all over our black, swastika, fuck-off T-shirts. It even started getting competitive, each of us trying to outdo each other with the biggest stain.

But like I said though, it didn't really catch on, I mean the goatees and the fucked-up biker look, that was a big success, Johnny Depp, Kiss, even Elton John, they all copped a bit of our style.

But for some reason the spunk-stained T-shirts never really caught on.

Funny that.

A bit close to home for most people I guess, maybe.

Being a wanker.

ONE INCH BABY

Harry was just one inch tall when he was born.

Harry is Robbie and Fiona's wild little boy. A flame-haired, elemental thing of six years old who swears like a bastard. I am proud to have been chosen as his Godfather.

This rock and roll thing, it's not all laughs, hi-jinks and mindfucking, buggery, drugs and Satanism you know. Sometimes the horrors of life, the fears and trepidations of reality are just too damn big to ignore.

Sure, nagging wives, bitching girlfriends, whingeing managers and the snakeoil queers of the Inland Revenue cosmosodomistic evil Empire, those fuckers are bad, but drugs and alcohol, sexual insanity and terrible, terrible groupie abuse can usually silence them down. Load up on enough badness and they just seem to throw themselves down the tourbus khazi.

But premature babies? I'm afraid even if he wanted to, there was no way Robbie could lob that one down the toilet of irresponsibility.

We were just two days into the tour when Robbie got the news. His unborn son Harry had jumped ship three months early. The poor little bastard was born one inch tall and with no lungs. Strapped in an incubator, touch and go, major fuck-off bummer.

Now as a band we were a pretty heartless bunch of rotten bastards. But even old Stargazer, the maximum Deep Lord of eternal darkness himself, even he could see the seriousness of this bum luck kick in the bollocks and remarkably – selflessly – suggested that Robbie get the next flight back home, to be with his Mrs and the one inch lungless wonderboy.

Tex mumbled about all the buggery and cocksucking he was going to miss out on, then added quickly: "But shit, yeah Robbie man, you should go home man." Trying to cover up his spectacularly selfish gaffe.

I must admit my first thought too was of all the Euro bumhole we were going to miss out on. But of course even I realised that Robbie must go home.

Robbie called the hospital.

Me, Tex and the Dark One sat around on the tourbus thinking about those perfumed petite French arses, winking down the Parisienne boulevards. Those statuesque Deutsche jacksies, tight brown swastikas begging for a little V2 KY action. Delectable, wholesome, Swedish iceflowers, clean as a whistle. Funky, musky, dark and dirty, those greasy, hairy Spanish bullrings.

In the freak-out galactica a swan infected 10 shards of the holy me boss with an unsane divinity

Zodiac

MARK MANNING

Sighing wistfully with rockets in our pockets but with our sense of honour unsullied, we put on brave faces. We were sacrificing a thousand scintillating girly shitlockers but it was out of a noble and manly loyalty to our brave musician comrade.

What great guys we were.

Maybe we could train up one of the roadies?

It can't be that fucking hard?

Yeah, it's only fucking drums?

None of these thoughts entered our noble honourable heads.

Besides, they didn't have to – Robbie, after an hour-long mobile phone conversation with his wife and several paediatricians, had decided to carry on with the tour. They would need all the money they could lay their hands on and Robbie would be of far better use to his new family out here than worrying away in England, the one-inch baby was in excellent hands, best doctors in England etc.

Not one of us breathed a sigh of selfish relief, anticipating that Pan-European avalanche of sodom with grinching penises, straining cyclops stylee in our filthy underwear.

"You're doing the right thing Robbie," said bad old Tex dreaming of winking bumholes, whipping out his bitchsplitter and slapping one off right there in the next seat to the worried father.

"Yes, there's not a lot you can do really Rob," added Cobalt sincerely. "The pair of them will be in the best hands of the whole of England." The guitarist cracked open another bottle of Jack and tryed hard not to do a highland fling.

I just smiled. "Hey Suzy Ringslinger baby, " I thought to myself, "Grease up them cheeks momma, the assmasters of the Apocalypse baby, oh yaass, we're comin oh yaasss... we is comminnn..."

Yet despite the Vesuvian streams of boiling dickmustard that we were ramming viciously up those EC jizzabelle bumholes I still couldn't help but notice Robbie's constant anxious trepidation. We all did our best to console him.

But somehow all the beer shotguns, crack/smack speedballs, the relentless buggery, Satanism and horrific groupie torture, it all just seemed to worsen things for the poor lad.

He just couldn't seem to stop thinking of his poor little one-inch baby.

A couple of times he seemed to forget, like when we got really gruesome with

146

a Czech whore, a firework and a big black dog.

But the next day like a stinky blue boomerang, his melancholia would be waiting for him in the bucket of vomit next to his bunk.

Even the usually insensitive American road crew from our fellow troubadours and support act Metal Church, had noticed Robbie's sad demeanour. "Whuzzup cuzz," said a huge American road gorilla. Tex had to translate, Robbie couldn't understand the ape's language. The big silverback's name was Lunk, he was as thick as shit but his heart was in the right place, behind his ribcage, near his liver.

We all kind of liked him, in a sympathetic sort of way.

Lunk didn't really converse, he just kind of made everything into some strange competition in which the USA always won. No matter what the topic of conversation was, old Lunk would steam in and tell you how bigger, faster, smaller, taller, thinner the same thing was back home in Shitsburgh Fatsylvania, or wherever it was the humongous redneck hailed from.

Subsequently in trying to lift the sad dad's spirits Lunk had informed Rob about how his elder sister's premature baby was only a *half* inch tall when he was born, "No bigger than your thumbnail, goddamit! But hell man! Now he's bigger than me, six foot goddamn eight, seven hundred pounds, plays for the goddamn Fatsylvania giants! Wooh!"

Robbie groaned and then started laughing, good lord, whose idea was America? The tour rolled on, Harry seemed to stabilise, but he wasn't getting any better.

We were in Rome and decided to pay a visit to the Vatican, the Pentagon of the Catholic church.

It was spooking me out big time.

Huge works of art you'd seen a thousand times in countless books and magazines. But the familiarity you thought you had with these sacred objects didn't fully prepare you for the stultefying awe these inspiring masterpieces seen altogether, *in situ*, whacked you with. These testaments to man's devotion to God were utterly breathtaking. I felt dizzy and small in that huge golden cavern with its writhing marble and shining oak. Heady incense, mangled saints dripping off the walls, hundreds of tortured Christs dragging their way endlessley around those gory stations of the cross, being scourged, mocked, tortured, everything short of being bummed alive before being thrown upon that evil piece of wood. The Powers, cherubim, seraphim, thrones, all the Angels and Archangels in heaven, flying around the massive Michaelangelo ceiling. Beatific Madonnas beaming all over the place rubbing shoulders with tearful dolorosas.

It was triple pant-shitting heavy, good buddy.

I remember thinking that if you said a prayer in this place and God didn't hear you then you had to be the world's most complete and utter fucking bad bastard – either that or God was deaf.

I've prayed twice in my life but didn't get a result, once for Josie's life after a car accident me and Evil had been in and once that I would get to cop off with Kate Moss.

I could see how the second request was pushing it a bit, but I thought the first one was pretty selfless, although I guess it could have been tainted with the fact that I knew that if she did get better, I was definitely on a promise. But even though my slightly tainted attempts at prayer didn't work, I knew that real prayers worked.

You just had to put in the hours.

I found this out by getting the poor sisters of Clayre in Lynmouth, a small order of Catholic nuns from a Devon seaside town to pray for me.

I was pretty much completely fucked on alcohol at the time.

I must have been, I was hanging around Catholic churches thinking of becoming a nun. It was a desperate summer, I was sat contemplating the sacred heart in their small chapel when I saw a rude wooden box with a notepad and pencil hanging next to it in a dark corner; a handwritten sign instructed the reader to write down his name and whatever they wished the sisters to pray for and to place it in the box.

I wrote down "My soul," and told them about the drink shit.

A week later I was sober for the first time in fifteen years.

Like I said, I guess you had to put in the hours.

But a thought occured to me in that giant dynamo of Catholicism. Maybe somehow your prayers were amplified here, like a giant holy Marshall stack with a direct connection to heaven, so loud that even a deaf deity could hear them. Maybe that was why Catholics made pilgrimages to places like this? Maybe your prayers jump the queue a bit if you worshipped in places like this?

I mentioned it to Robbie who looked at me as if I was nuts, he'd never got

down on his knees in his life.

What did he have to lose? I reasoned with him.

"Come on man, this is the Sistine chapel!" I implored.

"Prayers from a joint like this man, they must be louder than fucking Kiss!"
Robbie wandered off, looking at me funny.

A little while later I saw him wander into a small chapel off the main holy
headfuck drag, where he lit a half dozen candles, got down on his knees and
started praying like a motherfucker.

Maybe it was all the candles or something, coincidence maybe, but the next
day when Robbie phoned home, the one inch baby had grown overnight.

He was two inches taller and had grown a fucking lung.

Ave Maria, big time.

The power of love baby, don't fuck with it. Yeah.

ÜBERCHUMP

Pornography has been described by one eminent scholar as Art's dark sister. Something about how it is not only human sexuality that is revealed in those gory images of bumming, shagging, and tool-drooling, but how society itself, its fears, transgressions and general illusory nature, how they too are revealed amongst all the rampant boneology and onanism. Whatever.

I've lost the plot here, so I'll just bash it out and hope it comes back to me. Minutiae. Something to do with minutiae. You see I can't remember all the big grand stuff about being in a rock band. I can't remember saving little children dying from AIDS by wearing a red nose and making a cunt of myself in some fly-blown African shithole. I can't remember sending little Bobby Sockett a taped message to help him recover from his trash TV-induced coma.

I can't remember playing in front of twenty million people, feeding the world with the excrement of my overblown ego alongside my best mates Messiah Bonio and Saint Bobulous.

I can't remember buggering Indians and saving rainforests with my sage and deeply spiritual friend Johnny Bumblebee.

Nor can I remember saving little cuddly animals with that intelligent humanitarian Sir Paul McCrapney and his talented visionary genius of a dead wife, Loobie Loo.

I can't remember thinking that I was doing any of this rocking shit to save the world and help mankind at all.

But I can remember all the squalid petty little arguments, the cheap little bouts of oneupmanship, cruddy jealousies, predatory tattooed dogwomen, lousy food, vomitous back lounge rumble-thrones.

I can remember all the details about why rock *isn't* great. Why it has no noble epicentre to its being. Why it doesn't make people happy and bring them together. In fact I can remember all the shitty insignificant details that you, dear punter, never get to hear about, and you dear colleague would rather forget.

These crapulous details do not sell records you see, they do not contribute to the glamour that hangs onto rock and roll's venereal skeleton. These things do not even possess a tacky anti-glamour, like suicide and Empire State drug addictions, all that gory shit people like to read about in newspapers as some

kind of bogus amelioration of envy.

No, the only stuff I remember is the squalid pointless arguments and the pathetic games used to stave of the soul-numbing boredom of drug-dusted days sliding in and out of continents and consciousness, paying little attention to either.

Let me tell you about a pastime called chumping.

Chumping? You ask. What's chumping?

Chumping is basically a conspiracy amongst, in our case, three members of a band against the remaining member with the sole intention of making said remaining member look and feel like a complete and utter cunt. These can be short, harmless little affairs like say for instance, the conker chump. A jape played out on Tex, our unsuspecting Mexican/American bass player, who had little knowledge of English flora and fauna; or they can be long drawn-out sadistic affairs like the Blackout Überchump chump, both of which I shall explain forthwith just to show you how pathetic we sex god rock bands can be when travelling along that unforgiving tarmac, lost on all those autobahns into and out of Hell.

We were in some pleasant French town in Autumn, crossing a pretty boulevard, the rain had just stopped and had brought down a volley of horse chestnuts. The spiky shells had split and the lustrous nuts were rolling along the ground. The thing about conkers is that no matter how old you are, for some reason it is always extremely exciting when you come across these shiny treasures. It's probably got something to do with the hours spent fruitlessly searching for them, those tantalising shells way at the top of huge trees, throwing sticks at them till your arm aches, vainly trying to knock them down. I knew more than one kid who broke his neck falling from the branches of those towering arboreal giants.

Whatever. But here we were, me, Cobalt, Robbie and old Texyboy, grown men – sort of. "Oh wow man, conkers!" exclaimed Robbie bending down to pick one up. Tex, caught up in the enthusiasm grabbed one and looked at it quizzically. "What are they man?" he asked, obviously never having come across many conkers in Acapulco. "Like French nuts or something?"

It was almost telepathic the way that the three of us sensed an exquisite chump coming down as the dumb beaner stared at the alien object. Without even thinking Robbie, quick as lightning: "Yeah man conkers, they're like a French delicacy." And pretended to eat his conker. Cobalt joined in. "Mmmm delicious," he said.

"They're quite sweet for this early in the season aren't they?" I joined in.

"You fucking assholes!!" said beanboy throwing his half-eaten conker at Robbie. "I nearly broke my goddamn tooth you bastards!" Spitting bits of the bitter chestnut onto the ground.

Tex never really grasped the concept of the chump, probably because, being American, he was the brunt of most of them.

It must be an English thing, ridicule and humiliation. Tex just thought we were a bunch of limey liars.

The idiot tried to play a chump on Cobalt once, which completely illustrated his lack of understanding of the sadistic British tradition of taking the piss. Stopping late at night at some sprawling service station, Tex informed the snoozing Cobalt that that there was a McDonalds here and would he like him to bring anything. Cobalt put in his usual order for extra everything, extra large, with double cheese no gherkins and two extra large cokes with no ice then lay back to salivate. Some half hour later, with the sounds of Cobalt's burger-starved gut rumbling away in his bunk, Tex jumped back on the bus as the driver revved up the engine.

Hungry Cobalt peeled back the curtain of his bunk, sniffing like a myopic rat for his McFeast. "Tex," he called feebly. "Did you get my burgers?" he queried, looking worried.

"Ha ha man, I fuckin' chumped you!" laughed the Mexican, who thought he had finally got his revenge on the cunning chumpmeister guitarist.

"What?!" said the obviously angry and very hungry Stargazer.

"I fucking chumped you man, there was no McDonalds, ha ha, how do you like it you fucking limey bastard?"

Robbie and me were laughing at the pair of them.

"That's not a fucking chump, you idiot," said Cobalt, incredulous at beany's stupidity. "That's just a fucking lie," he added, stomach rumbling now, louder than the bus.

"You just chumped yourself Tex," laughed Robbie.

"What the fuck man, that was a fucking good chump man, what do you mean it was just a fucking lie?" said Tex, still unable to work out the subtleties of chumping, how it had to involve at least two chumpers to one chumpee, one on one chumping just didn't work. Chumping was definitely a pack, bullying kind of sport. Very British. "What do you mean just a fucking lie? That's all

you fucking bastards do to me all the time, just fucking tell stupid fuckin' lies to me, tell me that some Australian Rolf Harris guy was the first to record 'Stairway To Heaven', that Led Zeppelin just covered it, how good quality wines always have a screw top, conkers are fucking nuts and shit, fuck!" protested the confused Tex, not knowing what he'd done wrong.

Cobalt just looked at him incredulously and with a curt "Americans" threw the curtains of his bunk together and went back to sleep.

Me and Robb tried to explain the subtleties of humiliating and ridiculing one's friends, the point being to make the other party and not oneself look like a complete idiot.

But I don't think he ever really understood. This British cynical social cruelty being totally at odds with the genuine optimism and friendliness of his own have-a-nice-day culture.

But from these petty, trivial and failed chumps let me move on and describe to you probably the cruellest and most sustained and thoroughly evil chump of all time.

Who was the chump? Dozy drunken birthday boy Robbie the Vomit, heh heh, and what a chump indeed, one I shall never ever forget.

You would have thought Robbie would have known better.

I mean he was no wetback beanboy novice at this game, but oh no, the little Leicester skinwhacker walked straight into it, like a blind spaz, smack into a lamp-post.

It was the day after his birthday, so obviously the cunt was nursing a hangover the size of Mars. We were on that particularly foolish tour where for some reason we thought it would be a good idea to have Tennants Super lager on the rider.

Wrong.

As I've already warned you, Tennants Super is the purple-tinned shit that tramps drink. It has an alcohol volume of nine percent volume which is about the same as an average white wine. The thing is though that you don't drink it like wine. You drink it like lager. Fast and by the pint. It also has some otther weird shit in it called valerium, which is like some kind of dosser tranquiliser herb. So combined with cheap speed and his birthday celebrations you can imagine how fucked-up Robbie had been, he'd been surfing blackout miles per hour most of the evening, he'd shat his pants and everything.

MARK MANNING

We were all sat around backstage waiting for the crew to set the gear up, I'd cracked open an evil purple eye-opener and Cobalt was complaining about the sandwiches. Tex sat idly flipping through a magazine about bumming women.

I don't know where the idea came from, but it was inspired. "You don't remember do you Robbie?" I said quietly, my acting up there with sir John Gielgud. With stunning chumpistic telepathy Cobalt joined in immediately. "Don't Z, don't," he said, all concerned, the rat.

"What? What?" said Robb. Hooked. The Überchump was on.

"Carol," I said. Carol was our manager at the time and though not being completely hideous, she was no Kate Moss if you know what I mean.

"Shit, you don't do you?" I replied, appearing surprised.

"I was in blackout mode all fucking night, shit what did I do, I didn't fucking hit her did I?" the blurry-eyed chump replied, all worried.

Boy did we have him!

The first rule of chumpology, never admit to not remembering what you did when you were in megashiteface riding the blackout rollercoaster mode. By this time even old Texyboy had cottoned onto what was going down.

"Ha Ha, you don't fucking remember man, oh fuck!" he laughed throwing down his copy of *Anal Destroyer* #47.

"What? What?! What the fuck? What did I do, shit you bastards, fucking tell me!" His voice was escalating into panic stratosphere levels.

"Well I don't know if you actually...? Well all I saw..." I teased him, looking concerned, savouring his nail-biting, twisting hands. "Well, I just walked in the dressing room and you were like really slobbering all over her tits, you had them out and your pants were like round your knees, you didn't even notice I was there..." Lies, all lies.

"WHAT?" He shouted jumping off his chair. "Oh my God!"

"She looked like she was enjoying it though, she was groaning and grabbing for your bollocks..."

"You mean I fucked her?" he gasped, almost in tears.

"I don't know man, maybe you were just snogging, I left you to it." I compounded the yarn. It was Tex's turn. "You don't remember snarfing down on her pussy man in the back lounge?" said the evil Mexican. "Man it fucking stunk as well, you dirty bastard."

"I was sucking Carol's fucking cunt in the back lounge?!" shouted Robbie

almost fainting with disbelief and self-loathing. "Where the fuck were you lot?"

"We were trying to watch a fucking video mate, sucking her bumhole through the knickers and everything you were, fucking horrible," added Cobalt, sounding all offended.

"I had to go to my bunk man it was horrible, you were telling her that you loved her and everything, wanted to bugger her, you didn't even seem to be able to see us."

Robbie was as white as ghost spunk. He paced the small changing room, you could almost hear the machinery in his head spinning as it tried to unlock alcohol-fused memory circuits. "I wouldn't worry about it Rob, she was so pissed she probably can't remember it either," said Cobalt cruelly.

"Oh fucking hell, fucking hell, I'm a married man, what if the Mrs finds out?" said the loyal husband, head in hands.

"Well we ain't gonna fucking tell her man," said Tex helpfully.

"I don't fucking mean that, I love my fucking wife, not like you bastards!" he shouted throwing a can of the evil purple tin at the wall. "It's that fucking stuff!" He stamped on the tin, foam exploding all over the floor.

"Hey steady on man, you might not but we fucking like to fucking drink it," said Tex, picking up the crushed tin and sucking the foamy dregs from the bottom.

"Should I apologise to her or something?" said the reformed drinker.

"What for man, she looked like she'd probably be well up for a rematch, squirming away on your face like a fucking slug she was man…"

"Fuck off Tex, I'm gonna be sick." And he was.

"Fuck's sake Robbie! These are fucking suede man! You dirty fucking asshole!" shouted out the beaner as his new strides got a carrot shampoo.

Well this fucker ran and ran, Carol wanted to know what was wrong with Robbie, had she done something wrong, why was he avoiding her.

Robbie sat in the back lounge for three days biting his nails and looking perturbed.

Of all the sleazy individuals that have ever played with the Love Reaction, Robbie – although no fucking angel – was probably the most decent of any of us.

Which is why this chump was so fucking brilliant.

Robbie, who has been married to the same woman for nearly twelve years and still loves her. I mean even that should qualify him for some sort of canonisation, most blokes start plotting ways to murder their ball and chain in the first six months of padlock.

On and on it rolled. Cruel jibes about manager-bumming and public cunt-sucking, the poor bastard desperately trying to piece together those fatal blacked-out birthday-boy hours in his mind and failing. "I'm going to tell Fiona," he said at one point, Fiona being his wife.

"That's a really bad move man," said Tex.

"Yeah man, chicks're funny about that shit, sucking another bitch's cunt in front of all your friends," said Cobalt.

"She'll leave you Rob, believe me, I should fucking know!" I added cruelly.

"Oh God, oh God," was the last thing he uttered before crying.

Now a chump's a chump, I enjoy ridiculing and being cruel to people as much as any tabloid journalist but in the end, seeing that decent loving husband-type idiot in tears, I had to end this particular torment.

I told him we had made the whole shit up and, being the decent sort he is he took it like a chap and started laughing – more out of relief than anything else. Like I said, Carol was no Kate Moss.

Tex, the evil bastard, he reckoned we should have let it run forever, never told him the truth. Make him squirm for eternity.

Like I said, fucking Americans.

They really, really don't get it,

not anything,

ever,

at all.

NIGHTMARE AND HER HELLISH CLAN

JB's in Dudley.

To any poor unfortunate lager-drowned, speed-fucked bastard who has ever criss-crossed, pissed and incapable, the highways and byways that link England's black toilets of rock, this place needs no further explanation.

The mere mention of the name of this dreadful lavatory of warm beer, sticky carpets, scatological graffiti, black walls, unctuous gussets and feedback torture will bring a painful smile of recognition to all *fucked by rock* veterans of *The Terrible Game*.

JB's in Dudley.

Not just JB's.

JB's *in Dudley*.

For some reason the fact that JB's is actually in Dudley makes it even more funny, awful, sad and – in a strange way – almost noble. A shared hellhole, a shared dreadful experience that all British rockers no matter what their eventual status in the pantheon of rockness has had to experience.

Paying your dues I think our more sentimental and romantic rock forefathers used to call it.

Ask any seasoned rock trozzle where Dudley actually is however, and I doubt any of them will have the faintest idea.

"It's some place where they speak like it's Birmingham, but it isn't, isn't it?" is probably about the most clued-up information any of my decibelic bretheren will be able to offer you.

Dudley.

Dud.

A firework that doesn't go off.

A small damp squib of a town forged sometime during the industrial revolution that the world seems to have misplaced.

A place where the local accent is almost as indecipherable as in that other garbled vowel rape of the Queen's English, Glaswegian. A sing-song twang of a dialect not altogether without a certain anthropological charm that its townsfolk shout at you like a seriously tanked-up Noddy Holder.

The fact that that dreadful, dreadful, "comedian", the black one that married the fat bird, Lenny Henry, is Dudley's most famous son only compounds the horror of this blasted industrial landscape.

MARK MANNING

It could only ever hail from Dudley.

The most grotesque punter the world has ever seen.

Her name was Nightmare.

And she was.

She most fuckingly well was.

But before I regale you with more tales of rockish sordidity let me first tell you more about JB's in Dudley. The dressing room in particular, as that's where this grotesque incident unfolded.

To be fair to JB's though, really, on the the sliding scale of shittology, Dudley's miasmic jewel is probably no worse than most provincial rock shitholes. Those boxy black rooms where the paths of bands on their way up and bands who are spiralling their way back down on rock and roll's perpetual and inevitable trajectory invariably cross. Much humorous evidence of this dreaded curveball axiom is provided by the scatological insults left on the scary, spunk-splattered dressing room walls.

This is a funny little game of tit for tat mainly indulged in by the crews of bands, who all seem to know each other and have formed some sort of Hermetic brotherhood.

Because crew members have to earn a living and are not given free money by record companies, they often have to work for several different bands and therefore form quite large circles of acquaintanceships and friendships amongst their sweaty-arsed fraternity. (This is viewed with suspicion, mistrust and not a little envy by most members of bands whose insecurities and fragile egos have forced them into a tight incestuous relationship, trusting no-one and nothing from outside their immediate sphere.) Crew members check the lists of forthcoming bands and leave insulting, graffiti'd messages on the walls for following crews to read, great fun. For retard crew. Intellectual sensitive genius creative rock band boys however are above this sort of childish behaviour, and tend to use the pages of the rock press to trade their petty spite. Much more grown-up and creative darling lovie, don't you know.

So it was here beneath the felt-tip insults and badly drawn gynaecological illustrations that the monster from groupie Hell and her brother – oh my God, her brother! – manifested their incestuous mongoloid selves.

We'd just played another well-received gig at Dudley's premier lavatory of rocking and had lurched backstage into the cramped dressing room. We'd

been sitting around sweating for maybe ten minutes or so, the first bottle of whiskey had been decked and Cobalt was cracking open the second. Crew were banging around, slamming doors, shouting and threatening any punter who dared try to come backstage and politely say hello to the band. The room was slowly filling up with the usual backstage fug of sweaty bollock stench and fag and dope smoke, visibility down to about two feet. The bolder gash aggressively skanking their way past the crew's bad manners and into the squalid little room. Flash and Trash, as usual, like tumescent eels in buckets of swarfega were all over them, like flies on shit. Cobalt had struggled into his mingling gear – a fetching little military ensemble – and was heading out front to see if their was anything vaguely decent he could lure backstage, dose with Rohypnol and bugger to death.

I never bother making any cunt-related effort – it's a lead singer thing. The gash inevitably gravitates in a lead-singerly direction, the musicians however have to make that little extra effort and try to intercept the less determined ones.

The dressing room door slammed open, and there she was, this – this thing. Six foot two, albino, white eyelashes, pink eyes, everything, except she was kind of sexy in an end-of-the-world, after the apocalypse, fire and explosions kind of way. She was wearing a leather mini-skirt that barely covered her tight, eminently buggerable backside, ripped fishnet tights, a black bra, those pervy patent leather stiletto-heeled boots that usually only transvestite prostitutes wear, and nothing else.

Her brain-damaged make-up couldn't disguise the fact that if she hadn't been so obviously drug-ravaged, she would probably have been quite good looking.

For that brief second before she opened her big brummy mentaloid gob I kind of remember thinking something vaguely wistful and romantic about her,

the ghost
of pale beauty
hanging
fragile
on her
damaged...

something poetic and crap like that anyway. But then:

"Is thur a toilit in eyar?" she twanged, mentalist Noddy Holder style.

MARK MANNING

I noticed she was with another albino, male, obviously subnormal, he looked too happy to be sane. Grinning and drinking cheap lager with pink eyes. Gimpo mentioned something about how even us artists were having to experience the humiliation of defecating in the same lavatories as the general public, and no, there wasn't.

"Fook that, Oi can't use thim, thur all blocked oop int thoy?" said Miss Dudley Mental Hospital 89, pulling her pants down and taking a shit on the dressing room floor. "Yers dont moind does youse, but I was dying fur a crap, have you gorrany bog roll?"

I laughed and threw her some paper towels. Gimpo looked at me as if I was insane and threw a newspaper over the mad woman's small pile of black turds.

The albino dumpstress sat down next to me, her writhing pure white dreadlocks reminded me of LSD and Medusa. "Moi name's Noightmare," she said, and how appropriate, I thought. "That's me bruther." She pointed at the grinning sub. "Oi fuck him," she added and then she laughed, really mental like. A bit scary even.

By this time Cobalt had re-entered the room. "What's that fucking smell?!" he demanded.

"It's that fucking mental bird over there with Z," shouted the Gimp, "She just shat in the fucking corner!"

"Oi you!" shouted my new friend. "Don't be so fooking rude, I'll fooking clock you one, you coont!"

"Cobalt, meet Nightmare," I called to my guitarist friend.

"She fucks her brother," added Slam.

"Don't you?" Nightmare said, all surprised like.

"What? Fuck my brother?" answered Canadian drumming boy.

"Now, you stupid coont, don't youse fook your sisteh?"

It was one of those type conversations.

I tuned out and started in on the hard drugs.

It was quite unusual and out of character for Slam, he was usually, within reason, quite faithful to his wife, but I guess it's not every day that you get the chance to fuck an apocalypse, end-of-the-world, six-foot albino, mentalist dressing room dumpstress and her equally bizarroid brother.

He showed us the video the next day.

All three of them banging away in a mind-boggling knot of anal confusion,

animal and turd sex, fucking everything man, you name it.

Nice little Slammy and the Mentalists.

Wow, oh Lordy.

Slammy, he used to be such a nice boy.

ROOM FULL OF ROCK STARS

Now don't get me wrong. I've got nothing against drugs, or druggies for that matter.

My mother was a full-on pillhead during the sixties, raised two well-maladjusted junior delinquents whilst munching down on prescription drugs as if they were M&M's.

Valium, mother's little helpers they were called. They helped struggling working class mothers with two part-time jobs and wilful little bastard sons cope with the impossible demands being made upon them by the incipient advent of sinister, mind control advertising techniques.

All those invisible microbes lurking everywhere, trying to murder her family if she wasn't a good mother and didn't buy all kinds of bullshit variations of bleach that killed 99% of household germs. Didn't provide healthy nutritious Heinz baked bean bumholes and freshly frozen Birds Eye fish finger toenails for her two point four bundles of misery, not to mention providing an early morning sunshine bowl of niacin, ribofuckwhatever bogus vitamins contained in those healthy bits of flaked corn invented by that buck-toothed healthy sex farm pervert Mr William Kellogg.

So yeah, I guess if the doctor says they're OK then they must be. I mean, doctors man, they must know, they're the biggest bunch of junkie fucking crackheads around.

Look, if you kids out there want to take smack, crack, E, puff or whatever dumb little chemical it is that strokes your junior monkeys that's fine by me. If you think that you're like a kind of trainspotting, Ewan McGregor-type guy up on that big screen, running handsomely down some street with Iggy Pop lusting for life funkily behind you, great, except that I've never seen a junkie get off his arse once, let alone run skinnily down the street being handsome and rebellious in my entire life.

I've seen one or two fall asleep next to electric fires though, and wake up with third degree burns, but what the fuck, details, hey old guy, who needs them. And as for cocaine, now what a fine fucking narcotic that is. Guaranteed to make the user wittier than Oscar Wilde, as erudite as Jonathan Miller, the life and soul of every party, a whole fucking deaf room of the most beautiful clowns in the circus.

That's right, a room full of rock stars.

The time, nineteen eighty-something.

The place; some plastic simulacrum of reality out in the orange wasteland of the Arizona desert.

How do these things happen? How do three Leeds, Bradford, Manchester third-rate rock bands with scant connections to reality happen to end up in the same shitty piece of desert, on the same night, eighteen billion miles from anywhere?

There was either some seriously twisted conspiracy between management, record company and tour promoter, or the Devil himself was involved.

Some things don't bear too much scrutinization.

"Fucking Astbury man," said Cobalt, flipping through a copy of *Arse Torture International*. "He's down in the bar, dressed up as fucking Hitler or something."

The Dark Lord of evil guitarism chopped out another fourteen-inch line of white imbecile and hoovered it up through his single nostril, juddered and carried on his myopic inspection of women having their bumholes mangled.

"Ian? What the fuck's he doing here?" I said, snarfing up a similarly ridiculous amount of space dust. "The cunt." I'm from the North, insults are our way of showing affection.

I was genuinly fond of the Cult frontman, even if he was an arsehole – Jesus, I could talk!

I wandered around the labyrinth of corridors for a couple of hours, trying to find the bar, admiring the hallucinations.

I eventually found the joint, the usual flickering, shadowy candlelit shit that they always have out here in David Lynch territory.

The place was full of the usual plaid monsters. American alcoholics, vultures and sweating elephant seals. Serious skeleton twilight zone shit, dead-eyed, killer-knife trash and sweating fat guys with polyester shirts three sizes too small.

I scoped the room for Adolf baby, there he was at the end of the bar, lurking in the darkest shadow, slurring to Clint Dracula. What the fuck was Wayne Hussey, lead drama queen from The Mission doing here? Shit was getting weirder and fucking weirder.

I ordered a serial tequila slammer, slammed it and joined my rocktastic buddies. "So like, I did my sums, fucking April right, I was on fucking tour, the bitch... Z man, what are you drinking?" said Ian, not in the slightest bit surprised to see me, out there miles from anywhere in the Arizona desert. I picked up on the vibe immediately.

Rock maths.

How home bitch is up the duff and it can't possibly be yours.

Sad and eternal.

"What kind of idiots do these cunts take us for?" slurred Wayne.

"Fucking rich ones I guess," I answered wearily.

The womb, the womb, the nuclear weapon of a woman's sexual arsenal.

When this kind of misery is swirling around the dying beers and dead lemons there is only one thing to do.

Drugs.

Fucking mountains of them.

We pinballed through the spooky labyrinth trying to find the party. Whenever two or more rock bands are holed up in the same motel there is always a twenty-four hour party going on in some poor crew member's room. Four hours of bad alcoholic orienteering and we found it. Gimpo opened the door and the gale force intensity of sheer cocaine insanity nearly knocked us off our feet.

Drunken skanks impaled on all manner of sexual diseases, toilets full of fast food vomit and bloody turds, broken furniture, mountains of Columbian amnesia-dust blowing around like the Arctic.

"But I fucking love her!" It was Ian.

"Shit Ian, how many fucking kids have you got?" I made the foolish mistake of trying to console my rocking colleague.

"Three? four? Little Che, Tigerbelle Lucy Arse, I don't fucking know, how many have you fucking got?!" he ranted, tears welling in his drunken eyes.

"Look let's try and get this in perspective; first, how many wives have you got?"

It was hopeless. Rockers adrift in the twilight zone, it's like that alternative universe crap, the bizarro world in Superman comics. Everything upside down and back to front, the secret universe that I truly believe is closer to the truth than many of us dare consider.

Ian, Wayne, myself and the rest of our funky little wrecking crews were adrift on ridiculous floating islands of bad insanity that we only had ourselves to blame for. No-one forced us to do this shit. No-one told us to marry mercenary evil women with eyes on a meal-ticket for life, to become

sozzled imbeciles on tap for all manner of emotional sadism that these porno whores would continue to toss our way for the rest of our lives. Fess up dudes, we're dumb, we're stupid and we deserve everything we get.

That's it, I've lost the plot.

Again.

What a surprise.

Drugs kids, they're great, they make you have a fantastic time and never fuck up your life, make dreadful mistakes or kill yourself.

Take them all the time like big rock stars do and be super intelligent. That's my advice.

WIVES ON TOUR. WRONG

I had this great idea.

I'd get married and for the honeymoon I'd take my new wife on tour in America with me. That's how fucking intelligent I am.

Without fail everyone, including wifey herself, thought I was completely and utterly insane.

They were right of course; a few days after returning from probably the most emotionally devastatating six months of my entire life she had filed for divorce.

Brutality, mental torture, gross stupidity and being a complete rock arsehole being just a few of the eight thousand reasons she cited for getting rid of me. I couldn't disagree and gave her everything, what the fuck?

I guess I must have been in love, and as we all know, not only is love blind, it's a stupid cunt as well.

Everything appeared to be fine for the first ten seconds after we stepped off the aeroplane, but of course it didn't last.

I think it was probably Phoenix when something rotten in my leather trousers told me that maybe this hadn't been such a good idea after all.

Maybe I should have listened to Lemmy.

Lemmy, who hearing of my ridiculous plan had telephoned me to remind me of yet another rule of the rocking that I had never heard of. Lemmy acts as a sort of unofficial Godfather to all new rockers, an old Sarge-type cat, a veteran of many a dangerous campaign who is honour-bound to pass on all his knowledge of the arcane world of the distorted guitar and the blow job to inexperienced rookies.

Old Sarge Lemmy had told me that it was part of some rock code of honour that guys in bands were supposed to leave their wives and girlfriends at home when they went on tour so that all the guys from other bands who weren't on tour could have affairs with them.

Something about sharing, I didn't understand at the time, thought he was a pervert. But through the spermy mists of time and with a gnarled bell-end's worth of experience under my jock strap, I must admit I now have to agree with the crispy old rocker. It keeps the little lady's boilers stoked – and owing to the flaky nature of all rockers, there's absolutely no chance of anything serious developing.

But back to Phoenix, it was about our fifth gig and we were in this huge hotel with all the rooms overlooking this kingsize Disneyworld-type swimming pool, curly slides, underwater lighting, fountains, jacuzzis, fucking everything, all over the place.

I'm standing on the balcony looking down at the rest of the band and crew getting seriously sexually insane with a bunch of college girls. There's Cobalt buggering some huge-titted blonde in one of the jacuzzis. In the jacuzzi next to him, some slim redhead who can't have been more than about fourteen is getting a serious reaming from Cobalt's team bad buddy Slam.

Frolicking around in the main pool Flash and Trash are playing nude volleyball with about seven frisky nymphs, tits bouncing all over the fucking place, arses like little cherry tomatoes, bobbing in and out of the water.

The crew, Smithy, Joe, Gimps and a bunch of fat Americans are all gangbanging this cute little mulatto girl, she couldn't possibly have been more than twelve, cute puffy nips, flossy fanny hair. Smithy's bumming away on her tiny chicken butt, Joe's banging hard into her swollen mouth, choking the little cutie, some fifteen-stone Yank guy's banging hard into her cunt, a genuine airtight situation going down. The Gimp as usual is twanging away sat on her chest, aiming his pudwater for the youngster's eyes. Blinding girls with his ultra-acidic spunkslime was one of Gimpo's favourite sex tricks. Along with the usual arse torture, the Gimp liked nothing more than making young girls cry.

All this and the beer and the blow and the crack and the smack, what a fucking party. "What are you looking at Z?" said the Mrs, her voice had already assumed that black thundercloud quality, imminent rain on every parade in the world. "Oh nothing darling, just those idiots arseing around in the pool, God they're so immature," I said, seething with envy as I saw about three fourteen-year-olds start sucking Trash's dick, a couple of the other ones bobbing around sucking on the big fartbeast's bumhole beneath the water, snorkels and everything.

Flash was tit-shagging the famous West Coast stripper Busty Belle's 66" DD's like it was the end of the world. "Well come over here then and see what I'm knitting for you," she said.

"Oh that's lovely," I said, images of those lucky bastards having the gonad rides of their lives torturing me half to death. "What is it?"

"Yoghurt," she said sweetly.

MARK MANNING

"Lovely, what flavour?" What the fuck had I done?

"Muesli, your favourite."

As you can see by that last statement, I hadn't exactly been entirely honest with my new bride during our courtship. Muesli? I would rather shit my pants in the street than eat fucking muesli.

Now don't get me wrong, the Mrs wasn't completely ignorant about the ways of the rocking, she dated several rock and rollers before me, even that wild old heroin playboy Phil Lynott and one of the poncier members of Duran Duran. But these little affairs had all been off the road type things where it's a lot easier for us troubadours to conceal the true barnyard animal sides of our natures.

But out here on that flaming highway, it was pretty much doomed the minute we all got our visas.

Obviously it was the constant groupie attention that finally wore her down. And I mean we're talking American groupies here – pushy, professional, granite-hearted, fanny-farting, cum-belching überslags. Into the dressing rooms they stomp, wearing next to nothing, make-up trozzled on like transvestite hookers, silicon-enhanced buggery sockets, the works. "Hey Z, when you've finished with that tramp, how'd you like me to give you the best bumhole sucking through the underpants of your whole fucking life stud!" they would brazenly announce. "Actually you slut, I'm his fucking wife, and if anyone's going to be sucking his bumhole through his underpants it's going to be me, now fuck off you slag!" Wifey could hold her own, I'll give her that. I'd stand there sheepishly, almost apologetically, I had a strange sort of respect for these girls, I mean they provided a much needed service for us lonely musicians far from home. And if I pissed them off this time, what about when I came over next year.

I cracked in Reno.

Cobalt, Slam, Gimpo and I sneaked off into the neon and didn't come back for forty-eight hours.

It must have been the free whiskey and the fact that they didn't have windows in those places; the mud-wrestlers and reasonably-priced prostitutes didn't help either.

Three quarter of a million dollars in dollar slot machines, I wouldn't have thought it was possible either. But that's how much we won and how much

we spunked on that lost weekend skeezing beneath the neon. Seven-fifty K, and that's not even including the extras we tipped those vinegar-draining sluts round at Piss Flap Mary's.

Slam had come up lucky on one of the linked slot machines that they have all over Nevada, but it was way too far into our binge for him to do anything reasonable or sensible with it. We just poured it back into the machines, down our throats, up our noses. I reckon we got rid of at least a quarter of a million dollars up the arseholes of Mary's fuckpigs alone. But I can tell you fuck fans, it was a quarter mill well spent, oh yes sir, bumhole through the knickers indeed.

All this shit had happened well towards the end of the tour and relations between me and the wife had been steadily escalating into some kind of nuclear war. The screaming matches had rapidly escalated into full-scale domestic violence, which is pretty far out when your domestic situation is a tourbus shared with twelve other people. A couple of American guys had threatened to leave the tour when me and wifey had been laying into each other with broken beer bottles and karate, but Slam had straightened them out, explaining that what went on between me and the Mrs was none of their business, just personal shit. I guess that was true, but sometimes there was a considerable amount of collateral damage, civilians caught in the cross fire kind of thing, roadies taking beer bottles in the back of the head, the wife was a lousy shot.

So when I woke up surrounded by bloodstains you can imagine I got pretty worried. Where the fuck was the bitch, what was all this fucking blood everywhere? Where were my clothes? I wandered next door into Cobalt and Slam's room, similar carnage, broken furniture, blood and beer bottles everywhere, naked teenagers puking down the toilet. The usual shit.

Cobalt was asleep with his head beneath the air conditioning unit, icicles in his hair.

This was one of Slam's favourite tricks, dragging the comatose guitarist off of whichever groupie's arse he'd fallen asleep in and placing him beneath the icy air from those desert-strength conditioners.

The still-drunk drummer was watching *Sgt Bilko* on TV, a young girl was licking his knackers as he absent-mindedly wanked himself off. "Z man," he said casually, without taking his eyes from the screen. "What's up?"

I was looking under the bed and in the bathroom, checking the walk-in

Z ediac

closets.

"I didn't leave a body in here did I ?" I asked. The blood had unnerved me, I couldn't remember much about the previous evening and was casually trying to find out if I'd murdered the Mrs.

"Your wife? No man, she went back to England this morning, she told me to tell you that you were a psychopathic pig and that she was divorcing you, good news eh?"

Fucking excellent news I thought, as I slipped into a sleeping teenage girl's bumhole and took a swig of breakfast beer.

tattooed
beat
messiah

A KNIFE FELL OUT OF MY POCKET

Amsterdam.

All sleazebags love Amsterdam.

I love Amsterdam.

If sheer, end-of-the-world, horror sleaze is your bag however, Hamburg's Reeperbahn probably has the edge, being German and everything.

But you probably know that already, eh tugger?

The sleaze available in Amsterdam, I don't know quite why, maybe it's the friendly eager-to-please Dutch accent or something, but it appears to have an almost paternal, alternative medicinal type vibe, as if what you're up to is all perfectly normal, socially acceptable and healthy. Masturbating yourself into another dimension in a small black cabin whilst watching films of women having it off with fish. Buggering nine-year-old Arab boys half to death while their mothers stuff turtles up your backside. Having your knackers nailed to a wall by a fat old woman wearing a rubber mask, demanding the answers to long multiplication sums, you fucking name it. All perfectly normal expressions of human sexuality.

In Amsterdam.

"Of course. It is better to express your sexual side of your drugs and personality, no? Yeah, right, of course, would you like some hash? Of course, OK, yeah, great," says some stoned hippie policeman with a truncheon up his arse.

Pervert's heaven, and reasonably priced too.

So you can imagine with how much shock and sheer indignation I reacted when I was refused admission into these chink-bitch prostitutes' baggy bumholes.

I had the money, what was fucking wrong with them?

I had been doing the swarfega stroll, sleazing down chinkenstrasse admiring the fine Oriental merchandise. What fine class-A skank they were, sat there in their pretty little windows reading their *manga* comics and polishing their breasts.

It was mid-winter and the light powdery snow that wisped around my ears had taken on a magical, Disneyesque blue colouring from the ultraviolet lights in the windows. The whores liked ultraviolet. It made them look flat-toned, siren-like and extra alluring.

There was something wrong though, I noticed a look of trepidation in their shiny black eyes. Usually when surfing these tiny alleys of derangement and mad lust, the whores are more than eager to attend to the needs of that weeping cyclops lurking foetid in your underwear. Tapping coquettishly on their little windows, beckoning you in for a frenzied tonsil snarfing and savage, violent buggery session.

But not on that day, on that grimly fiendish day they looked worried, afraid even.

I thought maybe it might have been Joe, my six-foot-six ex-BNP half-caste roadie buddie. Maybe the sight of this humongous violence man was frightening the cute little Nipponese hornsmokers. I told savage karate, punter-dismembering Joe to hang back a bit as I thought he was frightening the poor innocent whores.

But no, every time I approached the window to try and do a bit of buggery business the girls would quickly shut the curtains and skitter back into their chintzy little shag parlours.

What was fucking wrong with them? I mean whores, they're supposed to have it off with anyone right? That's the deal. Bad breath, fat bastard, ugly, father-fucking perverted, turkey-spanking, worm-burping... any sad fucking bastard right?! You pay your money and you slam the slut, bugger her lungs out, choke her on dickslime, whatever takes your sick fancy. No questions, no complications, no stilted conversations, dinner, flowers, trips to the cinema or any of the other five million bullshit preambles to the grind. You just whack out your money and unload the pudslime in the orifice of your choice. So where did all this snobby closing the fucking curtain shit on me come from? Who the fuck did these skanky chink fucking bitches think they fucking were, the fucking Queen or something?

Believe me fellow lowlife paederast scum, there are few things in life that can make a pervert feel even lower than he already does than being refused entry into the baggy, shagged-out suppurating orifices of a whore.

What kind of subhuman creature must I be if Miss Yakamoto fucking Cashcunt won't even let me on board for a quick pump and a thump?

I stomped off into the neon, seething with anger and frustration, a tornado of misogyny and self-loathing. The fucking bitches, who the fucking buggering bastarding fucking hell did they think they were? I stopped off at a hardware shop to load up on a bunch of new knives. Sharp and shiny they

were, perfect for skinning sluts, chopping their ears off and taking out their eyes.

I couldn't understand it, I started shouting at Joe, asking him why he thought those slope cunts had drawn their stupid little buggery curtains on me. I mean didn't they know who I was! Darling! The singer in a rock and roll band! I was doing *them* a favour! Those slags should be paying *me*! Fourteen-year-old girls all over Europe would die to have me banging away on their virgin shitlockers! Rant! Rant! Rant! I seethed like Jack the Ripper all the way back to the hotel, almost in tears.

I ordered a triple tequila at the bar and decked it, quivering with rage. Gimpo noticed my perturbation and asked me what was wrong. Joe explained, trying hard to keep a straight face. "For fuck's sake Z," said the Gimp wearily – it had been a long tour. "Have you seen the fucking state of yourself?" he continued, ordering more tequilas.

"What are you talking about, you cunt?" I replied tersely, still angry, flicking the blade in and out on one of my new prostitute-murdering knives.

"Come over here and have a fucking look," said tour manager Gimpo almost sympathetically. We'd been on tour for over three months. Three months of suicidal partying, drunk beyond all belief and drugged way beyond sanity for pretty much all the way.

I stood in front of the full-length mirror and kind of got the gist of what he was saying.

I was dressed in a filthy chef's uniform I had found on the ferry, all the buttons on the shirt were missing, hanging open, the big spooky cross tattoo on my chest on full view, the flys on the oversized baggy denim chef pants were open and you could see my cock. I hadn't washed my hair for two months, it looked like a greasy vultures nest. My eyes were redder than Mars. Sandals, bare feet, it was snowing outside.

Oh shit.

A knife fell out of my pocket.

Oh dear.

Fucked by rock.

I slunk off up to my room, feeling ashamed, and slept for two days.

Fucked by fucking rock, again.

Fuck fuck fuck fuck. Rock rock rock rock.

THE CHOC VID

If there's one thing I hate more than anything in the world it's being hassled in a porn shop. The minge-dandruff bastards who work in those places. I don't know, maybe it makes them feel better, picking on innocent tuggers. Lets them off the self-loathing, low self-esteem rack a notch or two. "You must make a choice soon now, of course," says some Dutch arsehole wearing a purple polo neck pullover and grey leather trousers. I mean for fuck's sake, there's like nine million worm-burping mags in there, not to mention the twenty-five zillion videos. I don't think browsing for twenty or so minutes could be considered an impropriety.

So you can imagine how much I enjoyed it when the tables were turned on those filthy paedophile, coprophiliac motherfuckers when as a band we would descend mob-handed into their grubby little parlours.

I felt a little sorry for the solitary customers who scuttled out of the door empty-handed when this bunch of stinky leather-trousered rockers barged in through the wankistic doors and started guffawing loudly at all the depictions of the outer limits of human sexuality.

We were in Wankenburg or some other farthole of a place in Southern Germany. Bavaria, cultural home of Nazism, so it was all rather appropriate. We had a couple of days off so as usual the boredom factor had crept in and the porno videos were getting weirder; eels for pleasure, anal schoolchildren, regular depravo stuff. Gimpo was getting sick of it all and in his own unique way had decided to up the ante.

We were downtown. The Fuck Now boutique, I think it was called, a squat ugly old lesbian was sitting in the corner in jam-jar specs taking the tuggers' money. We were laughing good-naturedly at the child and animal porno-graphy when Gimpo wanders up to fatty tuppence licker and asked her where the shitting vids were.

Fat-arse gets all flustered; the tuggers rarely even look her in the eye let alone demand in loud voices information about which little corner she had hidden her spaccy tapes of people performing one of the most unfathomable wankisms known to man, the turd sex. The flustered lesbian creep nods nervously to a shady little corner, Gimpo strolls along and scours the wall. "Where?" he demands "It's just animals, pigs and stuff, baby-raping and stuff, where's the turd sex?"

MARK MANNING

The proprietress waddles over and points to the small selection. "Turd sex ja?" Even though it's her shop and she sells this filth, she cannot contain the contempt she feels for a man who is turned on by shite.

Gimpo knows this and for some weird reason it gives him a feeling of superiority, he has grossed-out the lesbian, cunt-sucking tugshop woman. We laugh loudly, unaware of the sly rotter's real intentions.

Back on the bus, the lousy bastard puts on his tape. *Best Of Choc.* Best of? Like this is the best? What the fuck must the worst have been like. The sleeve gave little away, the word choc was written in a kind of shiny heavy metal gothic typeface and there was a picture of a bird's arse. I wasn't really sure what was going to happen, maybe some bird kacking on a coffee table or something – but no, this *was* the best of choc after all.

We were all sat in the back lounge of the tourbus, drunk and drugged up as usual, Cobalt had cracked open a fresh bottle of Jack and Slam was chopping out the Charlie. Jack and Charlie, they're always there when it counts.

The shitty porn music had stopped and the jerky hand-held footage is in someone's back yard, ferro-concrete, East German cheapo vibe. An ugly junkie woman, red-haired with buck teeth is laughing and lying down on the cold concrete floor. A skinny pale-faced guy with a spotty arse crouches down over her face and starts to strain, his arse muscles osculating tightly. The back lounge druggy drunken debauchees fall silent, oh my fucking god, we seem to sigh collectively, I don't fucking believe this.

And the skinny acne boy's sphinc stretches open like a carp's mouth and this huge round boulder of grey shit flies out followed by a stream of brown water straight into the bird's mouth. Jesus fucking Christ, I could feel a ball of vomit making its way from my stomach up into my throat and bolted from the back lounge, down the stairs and into the bog, I hurled up my schnitzel into the chemical shitter and just about made it out of there before the Stargazer followed suit. Slam and Trash hurled in the front lounge, eyes watering and coughing like old men. We could hear Gimpo laughing triumphantly from the back lounge, the king of grotesqueness and insensitivity had triumphed again.

Gimpo was always doing this, getting one over on us.

He'd seen us laughing away at images of ugly women having it off with pigs and stuff, little kids and ugly old men, so the rotter had to go one louder. There he was proudly laughing away, showing how hard he was, even

shitting in women's mouths didn't gross out the King of the one-louders.

Gimpo had started playing it when we weren't expecting it. When we'd forgotten all about it and were watching rock vids or regular wanking porn, sitting around, drunk and stoned, guts and minds extremely sensitive, the bastard would have previously fast-forwarded it to the precise part where the greasiest, dirtiest most explosive squittering arse-bomb flies out of old Fritz's khyber all over the filthy fraülein's leering grinning chops. This as you can imagine was extremely traumatic; poor Slam had hurled his cookies twice when Gimpo had pulled this mature stunt.

You're sat there watching some regular tug movie trying to memorize the details for a sneaky bunktug later on when blam! your tumescence is torpedoed out of the sea of smut and sent straight down to porno Hell. We had to do something, it was starting to affect our minds. I'd be banging away on some pretty little road gash, coming up to the vinegar stroke when visions of choc woman snarfing down on Fritzie's logs would completely demolish my lobb-on and I'd be unable to do the business until I'd cleared my mind completely of the horrible vision.

I don't know whose idea it was, but it did the trick. When the regal überlord of gross-out was off swaggering about, bossing promotors and local crew around we decided to watch his vile choc video backwards, thought it might be funny seeing turds fly back up people's arses, backwards pissing, I don't know why, it was just something we'd never seen before. The weird thing was, once you had seen the film backwards its power of gross-out was completely and utterly destroyed. It was a vital lesson learned, a potent new talisman against the evils of Gimpology.

We sat there with great joy as the rotten little shit swaggered onto the bus and his face dropped when he saw that we were no longer affected by his precious little choc film. "Hi Gimps, come on in were just watching a movie," taunted Slam.

We all knew though, that Gimpo would soon find something else, something possessed of a profound evil, to torment and freak us out with. He was a cunt like that.

ECCE GIMPO (BEHOLD THE GIMP)
DRAMATIS PERSONAE #3: GIMPO

Gimpo, natural man, man of nature, a man free from the petty constraints of arbritrary constructs such as morality and religion.

A free man.

A Superman, übermensch, a man in harmony with his soul and the soul of the universe. A man with no shame, a man with no bird, a man of the wanking wounded...

"Go on Gimps, tell us about the hamster," said Slam, that's how it usually started.

The hamster was Gimpo's affectionate nickname for his then girlfriend.

So yeah, go on Gimps, tell us about the hamster...

"Yeah right," kicks in Natureboy. "Like I was like buggering around down on her fanny, giving her biffbat a right good fucking seeing to I fucking was, slurping around, pulling her pissflaps round me ears, as far as I could get them, when I decide to give her arse a good shagging as well, so I stuck my finger up to get her going and oh fucking hell!" shouts the Gimp warming to his tale, "There was a fucking turd up there, a fucking hard little pointy one, me finger stuck right in it, so I pulled it fucking out right and there's like fucking shit all over the end of me finger, God, horrible, so I stuck it up her cunt and slooshed it around to get it off, the dirty slag. You'd think she'd have a fucking proper dump before she got in bed with me wouldn't you? I mean she knows I liked bumming her. So I fucking finished with her the next day, the dirty bitch." This incident was obviously before our Neanderthal tour manager had refined his taste for all things turdological.

"Why do you call her the hamster Gimps?" Slam again.

"Cause her cunt smells like an 'amster's cage."

Or something like that.

How the fuck did the Gimp get to be the way he is?

Listen I've known this guy longer than anyone and even I still don't know.

I remember the first time I met him. I was shagging his sister, and he was home from the war.

Soldier boy, he'd just received a hero's welcome returning from that ridiculous scrap in the South Atlantic, The Falklands War.

A creepy and pointless demonstration of how deeply cynical and callous the

then Prime Minister Mrs Thatcher and her shower of sexually deviant underlings truly were.

Maiming and killing young men of both nationalities in a frenzy of jingoistic electioneering unparalleled in modern times for nearly two decades – until President Clinton decided to pull the the same sort of shit, bombing a bunch of babies during Spunkstaingate. Murdering innocents in an attempt to draw media attention away from his predilection for being sucked off by teenage gash.

Anyway that's besides the point. The Gimp and his gang of shell-shocked subs had returned to Blighty to be met on the docks by a bunch of tits-out Page 3 birds and eight million educationally subnormal Lady Diana fans.

Conquering hero Gimps obviously thought he had defeated Hitler entirely on his own. And the Vietcong, and the Japs, and all the other baddies he'd read about in his war comics.

That kind and compassionate newspaper, the *Sun*, had sent out thousands of those little black and white Commando comics that you find on rail station platforms to keep "our boys'" morale up. That's how stupid they thought "their boys" were. That somehow those barely literate tales of derring-do might somehow inspire Tommy on to acts of brave selflessness and sacrifice. Give up his life for privatised rail, electicity, gas, water, Sky TV and all the other really important things brave Mrs Thatcher, her brave ministers and brave Mr Rupert Murdoch were nobly scheming up back home.

Anyway Gimpo had returned home in his shiny boots, he'd won the war and so now he wanted his medal and to be given a fitting job for the hero returned.

But of course as every ex-squaddie, shivering on the Strand, homeless, strung out on smack or addled out of their sanity by alcohol knows, it doesn't always work that way.

England, in reality, loathes the lower ranks of its armed forces.

Especially the ones that survive her sordid little wars. They are a permanant and potentially embarassing reminder of the callous and scandalous ways Her Majesty's government treats the majority of its citizens.

Which is like shit, basically.

There is a popular misconception that the army trains young men to fight for their countries. This is and has always been, one of the most cynical and vile lies that Queeny and her arse-sucking spin-magician governments have been pushing for centuries. A soldier, a sailor, and more recently an airman have never been taught how to fight for their countries, they've always been taught how to *die* for their countries.

Without complaining.

Of course it's only when these poor bastards have been out in the field, sitting in a field of mud with fire and death raining down on them at all times of the night and day that they realise this.

On their return, as you can imagine, there are not a lot of jobs available where the skills required are an ability to roll over, get fucked up the arse by your government and die without complaining.

So the Gimp, on finding out that civvy street employers weren't exactly falling over themselves to recruit Falklands veterans who weren't even any good at dying – our hero got angry, very angry, very bitter and oh brother, believe me, triple twisted motherfucking weird.

Now while angry, bitter and twisted may not be particularly good qualifications for a job at the bank or building society, there is one job that is forever open to the angry, the bitter and the twisted. A willingness to die for something completely unreal and imagined, like a country, or a religion, to buy into something completely invented out of thin air? Even better soldier boy.

What job could this possibly be, you may ask?

A cop? A security guard?

No. Because of the anger, bitterness, and deeply twisted mindset Gimpo had been bequeathed by Her Majesty's treachery, there was now only one outfit that would welcome him to its manly bosom.

The Freikorps of the road.

Gimpo would become a roadie.

Not just any old roadie however. He would become a crack silverback with that awesome bunch of violent Neanderthals, those Nazi baseball bat-wielding thug motherfucking unwashed beerswigging speedfreak bastards, The Love Reaction rape crew. A Panzer death squad, arse-shagging division of glorious losers unparalleled in the entire history of debauchery since Caligula and his funky little Eyetie sodomites bummed and murdered their way across the entire continent of Europe.

Except that it didn't exist yet. But Gunner Gimp would see to that.

FUCKED BY ROCK

He would collect around him ex-forces psychopaths, homicidal bikers, deeply anti-social half-caste Nazis and ex-cons. The dejected and disaffected of all of England's nightmares would become the instrument of his terrible sodomistic revenge.

And all of England would pay for his dreadful treatment at the hands of Queeny and her sour milk government cocksuckers.

Oh, how it would pay. Especially the women. Especially the women and their pink little starfish arses.

Oh yes, cor blimey, bugger me, sir, oh yes indeedy fucking right matey boy... Gimpo indeed had all the twisted, compulsive masturbation, alcohol, drug abuse, sexually insane qualifications needed to become a prince, if not a king amongst that sordid and violent underbelly of the music industry. That world of dreadful, bad breath, cheesy bell-end blowjobs and unlubricated, painful, screaming sodomy.

That vile and terrible, cracked-mirror universe of hideously ugly, greasy, fat arse-crack, continuous toilet wanking, double sausage, bacon, egg, beans, mushrooms, fried slice, truckers dump farting scumbag lepers and grumbling pariahs, oh my god, oh my god... the world of the crew, the world of the the crew... aaaaagggh!

His lack of formal education and basic communication skills, whilst holding him back in most other jobs, were a positive bonus in this world of feral savagery and toilet sewage.

His tales of death, murder, war and rape. The atrocities he and his fellow British Tommys conducted beneath the gore-stained umbrella of the National Secrets Act.

Dreadful tales of disembowelled Argentinian boy soldiers, some no older than twelve or thirteen being forced to eat their own livers. His laughing account of the horrific rape-murder of the Downs Syndrome fish and chip shop girl – when over two hundred officers and men raped, sodomised and finally deep-fried the poor fourteen-year-old girl in her employer's deep fat fryer...

These stories inspired admiration and even envy amongst the wild animals whose duty it is to lift heavy things and direct electricity from walls into guitars.

Of course a man of this calibre was soon promoted to being the Love Reaction tour manager, the rocking equivalent of a general.

MARK MANNING

And that dear reader was where, as these tales obviously demonstrate, the
fun began...
The horror... The horror....
The bumming.... The bumming....
Gimpo.... Gimpo.......

SHY, DIRTY, AND STILL AT SCHOOL

Being in a rock band and shagging like a fucking monster for over a decade can tend to give a person a pretty distorted impression of women.

Especially if that person is pretty distorted himself to begin with.

I mean for ten years I used to think that all women were completely mental, that they were all slags and all of them without exception were totally evil. Actually I still do, come to think of it, but obviously that's entirely my problem.

I'm sure there must be some decent women somewhere, but you would never find them backstage at a Love Reaction gig that's for fucking sure.

Sometimes I wish I'd shagged more, really made good use of my stint at the trough, but I don't know, there was something tragic about a lot of these girls, tragic and not just a little sad. Most road gash is deeply damaged. Cobalt never had a problem though, he'd bone anything that crawled out of the mosh pit, breath smelling of the roadie's spunk she'd just sucked off to get a backstage pass, with an arse the size of China.

And as for Trash, Jesus fucking Christ, I don't think some of his special friends should even have been let out of their hospitals. Helen Back, that was one of old Thrustie's, a whole load of Rosie and then some.

I was a tad more picky, young and spectacularly pretty were my criteria.

So as you can imagine, I fell somewhat short of the million tally the old Stargazer managed to notch up. Slam didn't do so bad for himself either, although I seem to recall that he was often unlucky in love, the poor bastard seemed to have a permanent dose of particularly pungent gonorrhoea, old stinky bollocks we called him. I'll never forget the sight of him milking the custard out of his cock into some Danish slapper's drunken mouth. The band were going for a threes up, an airtight we called it, Trash was on the gash, Flash was up the jacksie and me and Cobalt had a tit each. A lovely young woman, Trash's girlfriend.

As I said my standards were slightly higher, I could never love a woman who thought it cool to get airtight with a bunch of STD rockers, I'm just funny that way.

Shy, dirty and still at school, that's what I liked.

There was one girl, Dandelion. A really beautiful young thing with legs as long as a tube train, I can't remember where or how I met her. I just remember this beautiful face like a French movie star, all petulant lips and chestnut hair. And these perfect legs that grew out of a pair of high heels and met somewhere in heaven.

I'd invited her to one of our gigs, thought I'd impress her with the lights and the noise, then back to the hotel for soft lights, gentle music – and savage buggery.

She came along to the show on her own, and seemed a bit overawed.

I seem to remember that she wasn't your average rock chick, roadie-gobbling backstage leper dog woman, and conditions backstage at the London Astoria seemed to intimidate her slightly. I mean it was all perfectly normal to us, drunken bikers bumming schoolgirls in the toilets, people jacking up heroin into their eyeballs, lots of loud farting, but it all seemed a little much for poor Dandelion and so she got so drunk she could hardly stand up.

I don't know why but this somehow endeared her to me, there's something about a paralytic woman that makes me want to look after her.

We went back to the hotel and had the usual drunken sex, she didn't want to suck me off, which I found cute. My knob does smell like the North Sea though when I'm gigging, so I didn't push it.

She would probably have thrown up anyway, she was so ratted.

I was obviously impressed by her though, as I arranged to meet her later in the week at her place.

A rare thing for a rocker.

Fuck 'em and chuck 'em, as we say in the business.

Her council flat was right next to a sewage plant.

Not good.

I do find the smell of shit quite off-putting when I'm banging a bird.

I shut all the windows and got down to it.

The usual stuff, legs all over the place, grinding and drinking and grinding and drinking.

I got off her after about the third time and nosed around her bathroom, the usual potions and lotions young women collect in their boudoirs.

The place was quite pleasant apart from the lingering smell of shite, but there was something else I couldn't quite put my finger on.

A kind of melancholy dustiness and the presence of another.

Shit lying around that wasn't female. Little rubber skeletons, pint pots, man things. A razor in the bathroom.

I noticed the photos, some young man with blond hair smiling.

There were several more of blond boy with Dandelion on holiday in Greece or Spain or some other package joint where young people with not much money go to. I asked her if it was an ex-boyfriend, worried slightly that it might be her current one.

I hate shagging other blokes' women, it's a cunt's trick.

I only ever did it once and the bastard fucker tried to kill me, seriously, hanging around outside my house with a knife and everything.

"Yeah, he died though," she said.

"Bummer," I replied, feeling that all of this was going wrong. I don't know. Death and the smell of human faeces, not much of a turn-on.

"Last week."

Fucking hell, the poor fucker wasn't even in the ground yet and here she was banging Johnny Bastard.

I told her I was going out to get some fags and fucked off home.

I mean fucking hell, I know I'm a cunt and stuff, but I would like to think that if a loved one of mine ever popped her clogs I'd mourn a little longer than three days. Good Lord, respect for the dead or what.

Of course the old king of the thrusters, bacon sandwich sexboy Trash had no such moral quandaries and was straight in there.

"Did she suck you off?" I asked Spunky Sam.

"Oh aye," he replied gallantly. "Finger up the arse and everything."

Women.

Fucking evil.

All of them.

Especially the good-looking ones.

stars blazing behind
mad eyes,
we descended to earth
in a broken cadillac drawn
by swans.
we crafted music from
the air
and scattered it across the
teenage frequency.
we were born in the fifth
dimension,
the twilight goddess pays
our wages.
tell the government
the love reaction
wants the world.

BALLS AN' ALL
DRAMATIS PERSONAE #4: TRASH D. GARBAGE

"No, listen right, I'm not fucking joking, right, I'm fucking drunk now right, but tomorrow right, I'll fucking have you Smithy," said Trash in some hotel. The pakistani Elvis impersonator and bass player for the Love Reaction was slurringly, droolingly, head-noddingly, deludedly drunk.

Of course he could engage in a fist-fight with the human tank, biker psychopath guitar tech *(not a roadie, Smithy was definitely not a roadie, he wasn't even crew. He was a guitar tech. Road politics, sorry)* and kick his arse. Yeah right.

They don't make them like Mr Trash D Garbage any more.

Thank God.

I was genuinely fond of the old thruster, he seemed to live in an entirely different universe from everyone else.

Maybe it had something to do with the fact that he didn't do drugs.

Well, he *was* partial to the odd mile of cocaine – but only as an aid to drinking.

Cocaine for serious degenerates is only ever an aid to drinking.

To understand old Trash boy, first it is important to explain that he was a dyed-in-the-wool Yorkshire bazzer.

A Yorkshireman through and through, he drank Tetleys bitter like water and duffed up his wife. Except that he didn't have a wife – but I'm sure if he did have one, he would definitely have duffed her up.

It's what Yorkshire women expect.

If you don't beat Yorkshire women regularly they think you're a poof and leave you.

I too hail from that huge bleak county, so I know what I'm talking about.

Let me explain a few things about Yorkshire, that spiritual home of the biggest, meanest, rottenest, sexiest bastard that ever drank beer, farted and beat up his wife in the history of literature ever.

Potent, spunking, bitter-drinking Heathcliffe; a nightmare Oliver Reed sex beast. Shagging women all over the place and treating them like shit, a collective Yorkshire female fantasy dreamt up by a tiny Howarth virgin called Emily Brontë.

Heathcliffe *is* Yorkshire bloke.

Bad-tempered, full of himself, a foul-mouthed cocky bastard, contemptuous of everything except beer and his penis.

Beer and shagging is all Yorkshire bloke is bothered about.

Fighting's OK too, but it's a bit strenuous.

Sport, football and that, it's not bad, but in Yorkshire reality, all sportsmen are poofs. If they weren't they'd kick the fuck out of the ref for telling them what to do.

A popular joke amongst Yorkshiremen speaks reams about the psychological make-up of the Pennine beast. I can't remember it exactly, but it's something about the perfect woman being only three feet tall with a flat head, so that Yorkshire bloke can rest his pint on it when she's sucking him off.

Yorkshire, I love it.

What does Yorkshire bloke think about the rest of the world, politics, all that bollocks?

Anyone south of Yorkshire is a poof.

The North?

Yorkshire *is* the North.

Jocks? Scottish? Fucking animals.

Irish? Thick cunts with bombs, jessies scared to get it on with their mitts.

Welsh? Sheep-shagging runners hiding out in mountains during invasions, they talk fucking weird as well.

The rest of the world? A bunch of losers too stupid to learn how to speak Yorkshire.

The whole fucking lot of them, a bunch of bollocks.

Except for Australia.

Australia.

Australia, the promised land.

Sun, beer, fucking loads of it, cold an' all.

And Sheilas.

Sun-tanned birds with big tits that do as they're told.

Australia is the only country, apart from Yorkshire, where they play rugby league.

Rugby league, the only sport where the ref keeps out of it and lets the violence roll.

Rugby league is just fighting, with a squashed football thrown in to somehow make it look like sport.

MARK MANNING

Excellent.

This was Trash's cultural heritage.

No wonder I loved him.

The big stinker.

Except that you have to understand one thing.

Women.

They rule.

The tragic truth.

In Yorkshire, women are the boss.

I'm telling tales out of school here, but it's the truth.

Yorkshire is matriarchal.

Men, big coal-mining men, big farting bastardboy men, tough as brick shithouse men, all of them, hand over the wage packet.

And get pocket money like schoolboys.

They headbutt coal faces, grind themselves into arsecrack holes in the ground, whistle insults at schoolgirls.

But always, it is she who must be obeyed.

With a rolling pin and a face like thunderclouds, that rains on every parade in the world.

Mother.

Which brings me round to balls an' all.

Oh Trash baby, I apologise.

But here it is.

Big John Cockworthy Trash boy was relaxing in the back lounge, can of beer in one hand, pint of Jack and coke in the other, cigar in the ashtray.

The Yorkshire lunk was feeling expansive, he'd had a ten-mile line of cocaine and he wanted to talk.

About his amazing sexual prowess.

Trash boy hadn't been in the band long and the transformation from mini-cab driver to bass-toting, love-god sex-machine had been, to be quite frank, frightening.

He'd done all the usual shit, fucked anything wet, dumped his long-standing girlfriend and got himself a well-stacked fine piece of high-heeled heaven.

"Fucking hell, my bird right, Jasmine," said the low-rent Lothario, the Halifax seducer, the Yorkshire Don Juank talking about his new superbird. "She's fucking great at sex, fucking filthy she is."

190

"What do you mean, Trash," said sneaky Cobalt. I could sense a wind-up, a major chump coming down ultra rapido, so I paid attention.

"Well, not only does she let me bum her as much as I fucking want, all the fucking time like, but when she sucks me fucking cock, not only does her mouth goes right down to the root right, full on fucking deep throat shit and that..."

"Yeah, go on." Cobalt again.

"She gets me fucking balls in an' all"

"What?" laughed Cobalt, spitting his pint of Jack and coke out. "Balls an' all?"

I mean, come on, it is pretty impressive, even I have to admit that.

"I know, I couldn't fucking believe it meself, I thought she were gonna fucking eat me alive," said the king of fat sex.

"Sounds fucking scary if you ask me, what if she'd have fucking sneezed or something, your bollocks would be like an anchor, like dogs when they get tied, and she'd bite the fucking lot off," I prompted, crossing my legs.

Now a gentlemen does not speak about his ladies in front of other gentlemen. But none of us were, by the wildest stretch of even my imagination, gentlemen.

"So Jasmine," I said at the hotel bar. "Is it true then?"

The look on Trash's face told you that he knew immediately what I was going to say.

The colour from his big beery face drained leaving him fish belly, ghost sperm white.

"Trash says you get balls an' all in your gob."

Imagine the blackest thunderclouds that ever sailed across the horizon, lightning bolts flickering out of them twenty miles away.

That was the look she narrow-eyed down on old Trashboy.

Kiss and tell.

Balls an' all.

Oh dear.

Dumped.

Uncere-fucking-moniously.

SWAPPING SPIT

Entering the period of life where you start getting nostalgic over sex, for the time when you used to enjoy it. The tragic phase. Strange reveries visit as I lie here enjoying the sensation of gravity as the water drains from my bath. I watched the Larry Clarke movie, *Kids*, maybe catch a fleeting view of illegal tit. You know what I mean, when they stand up on their own.

A thing so temporary, maybe two years or three.

Like a rare bird that visits before high-tailing it down to Africa.

Well there was none of that, Larry deployed the mermaid technique, long thick hair draped artfully across Lolita's budding nips. Bastard.

But what his film did explore was those kisses that last for hours.

Virgins with sweet breath, boy and girl, both of them, tongues intertwining till their jaws ache.

Whores are extremely reluctant to offer this service.

You can fuck them up the shitter to your heart's content.

But kisses are for lovers.

This has always been so.

A real kiss is not for sale.

You are old and your breath smells of your last meal.

Your teeth are yellow like a dog's.

Is it any wonder?

The years file by, cunts give up their wet velvet for your increasingly jaded dick. The pleasure of a kiss that lasts all night becomes long forgotten.

The first time your fingers get wet, from then on, cunt is the object of your campaign. The kiss is the first casualty of the genetic imperative.

A long-forgotten pawn in this mad game.

Of course there are sensualists among us whose insane ardour fools even themselves. Amateur Lotharios who probably read things like this hoping somehow to improve their technique. How gross.

Fools who never knew how to love in the first place.

Sex, like love is only successful when both lovers are entirely selfish.

A considerate lover. How deeply unarousing is that.

A cunt sucker, a little dog trying to please his mistress.

A woman's orgasm is debased by men like this.

A woman's orgasm should be a rare thing.

How much more meaningful that shudder then becomes.

When love enters this savage rut and sends her to the stars.

No condoms or women's magazines, or any of the other tawdy shucksters who steal the energy of this precious thing and try to sell cars on its purloined, dead back.

There is no such thing as casual sex.

It is a lie conceived of by deeply insensitive fools who are trying to sell you something. I am not saying it does not exist, merely that it is worthless. An act of civil obedience whose conditions are dictated by the idiots who write women's magazines.

As a fucked-out rock and roller who has enjoyed a fabulous rainbow of gash – from the palest pinks of Northern Europe to the deepest purples of the African rainforest – I know what I'm talking about.

Scandinavian girls whose white hair smells of snow and poetic desolation.

Mediterranean women, beneath prussian blue nights, stars jangling, lost in the thick scent of night blooming flowers.

American women, where love is under constant attack, whipped by a whirlpool of mendacity and shadows.

And how beautiful is the first kiss?

An exploration of another's soul.

Tentative and serious.

Is this the one?

Is this love?

Tasting each other.

Is this the flavour I want to spend the rest of my life with?

Make babies with?

It is not only youth that is wasted on the young.

THE LOGGER
A ZODIAC MINDWARP MYSTERY

Gentle tugger, the terrible tale I have to tell you now is all completely true. A ghastly, stomach-churning story of mystery, paranoia, supernatural dread, and shit.

It was another of those dreadful tours of duty, rocking our minds into premature senility. All morals and decency shaved away from us years ago. So what's new? you might ask, "You're always telling us how depraved you are fucker, get on with it."

OK, OK I know, but I have to set the scene to create the green miasmic steam of gut-curdling paranoia, the fear and loathing. The are-we-all-going-mad? vibe.

It was like that movie, the remake with Kurt Russell, John Carpenter's *The Thing*.

Which one of us was it? Everyone denying responsibility, suspecting the others of the foul deed.

Which dirty, fucking bastard had shat in the tourbus chemical toilet?

Now, rock and roll, especially the soul-destroying, liver-shivering brand we were embroiled in, traditionally has little, if any rules at all. Except this one. You never, EVER shit in the bus toilet.

It is strictly for pissing gallons of beer into.

This didn't just apply to our bus. This was the rule throughout the entire headbanging fraternity of fucked-up rockers everywhere.

Not only rockers either – even Kylie Minogue's perfumed little fairy turds, they too are strictly *verboten*. That cute Elastica chick, what's her name? Justine. Why do you think they took so long too make their last album?

Suspended sentence, three years. Caught shitting on the bus, some reckon if it hadn't been for Albarn's money she would have got life.

The reason behind this harsh rule is the festering gut-churning stench, slithering around the bunks, like a spoiled eel. God, can you imagine if Lemmy ever shat on the tour bus. It would be an international incident.

Nope, dumping was only ever allowed at motorway services or at gigs. This meant that at every service station we would all strain as hard as possible, piles bursting like cherry tomatoes under a jackboot all over the fucking place. Moaning and terrible screams of agony echoing around the tiled

cubicles.

The squittering sounds of serious pebble-dashers, diarrhoea exploding all over the back of the Armitage Shanks. The deep resonant sploshes of particularly reluctant constipation boulders forced, squeezed through the gates of Hell. The awful sound of oxtail soup unloading at a hundred miles an hour, pissing out of your arse like a high pressure water hose. I'm not going to even talk about curries, chillies, ring of fire, you know what I mean. God only knows what any normal traveller unlucky enough to be in the same motorway bogs thought of the wailing and shouting coming from the four toilets.

"Oh God! God! Out Beelzebub! Out!" Dinosaur farts, like distant thunder, echoing around the anal torture chambers. But it had to be done, even a few rabbit pellets, the next stop was twelve hours ahead, and God, I'm sure all you kegshitters out there know what the agony of holding onto a heavy load for even half an hour is like.

It was me that found it. I stumbled, still drunk at eight in the morning, down the small staircase and pulled open the bog door. I couldn't believe it. Not only had the fucking criminal dumped in the bus shitter, he hadn't even tried to cover up his crime, he hadn't even flushed it. There it was in all its horror, a skinny coal-black turd. It was as if the guilty fiend was taunting us with his criminal audacity.

Now this might sound funny to you who've never lived on a bus for months at a time, but this was one serious fucking crime.

I rushed up the stairs shouting at the top of my voice. "Cobalt! Suzy! Robbie! Quick! Get up, some one's logged in the shitter!" My heart pounding.

"What!" cried Cobalt, pulling back the curtains on his bunk.

"Fuck off!" said Robbie in disbelief, pausing his eight millionth attempt to bring down Goro on his *Mortal Kombat* game.

"I don't believe you," mumbled the permanent pothead Suzy X.

"Fucking come and have a look! I tell you man, someone's fucking logged!"

We crowded around the small toilet, "Fucking hell!" said Robbie. "They have as well," added the weary *Mortal Kombat* warrior.

This was serious. More serious than ever, when no-one admitted to this hanging offence. The paranoia-like forked lightning grabbed us in its leather glove and squeezed hard. There was a logger amongst us.

MARK MANNING

For the next four days this was the only subject of conversation. Accusations and denials flew around the bus. Screaming, tearful denials. Suspicions and conspiracies abounded. Who was this monster, this Jack the Shitter? I argued that it couldn't be me, as I'd found the dead turd. "That could be just to put us off the scent," said Robbie, his eyes screwed tight with cunning as he pointed at me. "Yeah," said Cobalt, "That could be it, trying the old discovering-the-body trick," he added, slowly nodding his head.

"No way," I retorted. "The turd had dried out, it was at least four hours dead. And anyway I would rather have shit the bed than break this iron law. Shunned for the rest of my rock and roll years as the guy that shat on the bus khazi.

This bogshite Cluedo rolled on and on. Who was the culprit? I tried to piece the evidence together, like a rectal Sherlock Holmes, racking my brains, trying to figure out who hadn't dumped at the last service station. But we all had, the four of us, grunting and crying in adjacent cubicles. What had everyone eaten for their last meal?

Robbie, being a vegetarian was pretty much in the clear, since veggies do little yellow pellets, like rabbits. Well that's what I imagine them to do at least. This skinny black-snake creature was as black as dried blood. Definitely the log of a carnivore.

My bet was on Cobalt, it's just the sneaky little thing old foxy Stargazer would pull. If only for the pleasure of lying about it, one of his favourite pastimes. Cobalt was infamous for his pointless pathological porkies. I was convinced.

"Cobalt! J'accuse!" I shouted after my second bottle of blue label Smirnoff.

"Yeah, Cobalt! I reckon it was you as well!!" added Robbie, rounding on him like a pack dog.

"Fucking logger!" said Suzy, joining in the hysteria.

"This is a witch hunt, I swear it wasn't me! My shits are fucking massive, at least three times bigger than that skinny little fucking thing!"

He had a point.

On the fifth day, I was sat backstage still trying to deduce the culprit of this dreadful crime. If this matter wasn't resolved soon, we'd have to call in The Yard.

As I sat there perplexed and troubled, the door burst open; it was Cobalt and Robbie, they were breathless, the dressing rooms were on the third floor.

"He's confessed!" shouted Cobalt jubilantly. I was confused.

"What, who's confessed, what are you talking about?"

"Suzy!" shouted Robbie. "He did it!"

I was still confused.

"The Log!"

I cursed under my breath, it was all so obvious. He ate like a bird, that would explain the meagre dimensions, all that hashish. Fucking obvious.

"How did you get him to confess?" I asked, genuinely impressed.

"We just kept going on at him, till he snapped!" said Cobalt smugly.

A shame-faced Suzy skulked into the room.

"I'm really sorry," he mumbled. "I couldn't wait, I was stoned, I thought I was at home on my own toilet. It won't happen again, I promise." His bottom lip trembled, he wiped an eye with the back of his hand.

The sentence was lenient.

He got kicked out of the band.

Diminished reponsibility, owing to the half acre of skunk he got through in a week.

Dishonourable discharge.

He would never work in show business again.

THE DEADLEG

Now I know all this talk of punk rock bitch-buggering, groupie abuse, thousands of square miles of every drug ever discovered in the vast rainforests of fucked-upness, mammoth, insane, methedrine-fuelled masturbation sessions, locked in German tug cabins for days on end, wanking to limits of endurance and insanity that would amaze even the hardiest and most pointlessly stupid, sledge-dragging, polar explorer and his weird mountaineer cousins, drinking that would shame a Viking berserker, pant-shitting becoming as normal as vomiting and pissing yourself at teenage cider parties, all the mindless, pointless and brutal, horrific violence – I know it sounds like any normal, healthy teenage rockhead's idea of hog heaven, but well pards, I'm going to have to disappoint you a little. Not much, brothers and sisters of the power chord, it's still probably the best job in the world ever if you're fourteen. But not all of it is gravy. Now don't worry believer, I'm not going to bore you with all that horseshit whingeing pedalled out by the lesser mortals of our noble craft. "Oh it's so boring, hotels, hotels, loads of spare time two hours on stage," you know that pathetic ungrateful shit those softie little indie bands, missing home and girlfriends piss on about. You are a disgrace to the Rock! Hang up your plectrums and retire to a pathetic hobby farm RIGHT THIS MINUTE! Go and do some tantric knitting with an ugly wife, go save a rainforest, buy a pet Indian. You fag!

Get into ridiculous, fatalistic Indian religions, or even better, dig ancient kike bullshit kabala bollocks. There are a million ways to make yourself look ridiculous and demonstrate your deeply shallow intellect apart from just wearing sunglasses indoors. Pinhead women of the rock, go for it, get out of here you shameful creatures. Go hang out with some pet shop boys! Good lord.

Where was I? Damn, it's good to rant now and again, especially when in your heart, in your blood, in your nads – especially in your nads, the spiritual home of the rock – you truly believe in the sanctity and sacredness of joyous, manly rock and roll.

Buddhists believe the gut to be the bodily location of the soul, stupid Chink fuckers, what do they fucking know, chanting and smoking joss sticks with finger cymbals up their arses.

Soul, balls. Remember that rockers, and it will serve you well should you

ever earn the right to stand on the hallowed stages of rockness.

But as I said there is the one thing about all this rocking that no band, not even the truly, truly great ones – ones like, well, like us I guess – cannot avoid, and it's a real pain in the butt. It's a pain in the butt, but it can result in some truly awesome moments of staggeringly hilarious rock and roll arseholeism that make the pettiness and unrockish nature of this thing almost worth it.

I'm talking about the bickering.

Despite our onstage image of unrivalled testosterone-fuelled hyper manliness, the terrible truth is that without exception, I'm afraid all rock and roll bands behave like girls most of the time.

Bitching about other bands, getting the hump about the most unbelievably petty things imaginable. Shit, I shouldn't be telling these tales out of school really, but fuck it, no-one else is going to. Did any of you fuckers know by the way that all of Lemmy's friends call him Gladys? Thought not. I'm known as Shirley by my rockular intimates, and the Stargazer's *nomme de guerre* is Bunty.

Rock and roll is not particularly well known for having literary snitches amongst its Neanderthal ranks. Let alone writers of my undeniable genius and calibre. Listen, if you don't like it, just fuck off and write your own pathetic crap, you weed.

Oh my god, the bickering. You wouldn't believe it. Especially as within our ranks we contained one of the biggest bitches of bickersomeness the world has ever known. I'm talking about Queen Bitch himself, little Tommy Quarrelsome, Fanny Argumentative, rubbish dribbler, arguing the toss while tossing, that scatfreak, buggering, blur-fisted, moaning fucking cunt of all B.C./A.D. eternity.

Fucking Gimpo. Lady Grizelda herself.

Despite his undeniable qualities at violence, drugging, drinking and buggering the shivering livers out of some of the ugliest women that ever walked this fat-arse planet, the Gimp – what a fucking bitch.

It was relentless. Constant twenty-four hour piss-taking, shit-ripping insults. Arguing. Moaning. To tell you the truth I almost, *almost* I stress, felt sorry for some of those thieving weasel promoters one has to unfortunately deal with in this sordid business of tantrums, beers and tiaras.

Gimpo made our lives almost unbearable for the pettiest reasons. But the

MARK MANNING

Hi, I'm Shirley

shit he threw at those poor bastards. It was beyond sadism.

You'd have to invent another term entirely for the petty bullying he inflicted on those poor criminals, whose only crime was to try and scam money off a bunch of stupid chimpanzees with guitars.

Threatening to pull gigs if the clean towels weren't cold, if the rider was not presented in an attractive display. The flowers not fresh enough. And if the beer wasn't at least five percent volume and chilled, well that was it, show cancelled.

All this shouted at ninety-five decibels, his hearing aid squealing feedback.

It was also delivered in Gimponese, Gimpo's own special language, where all the words of a sentence are fired out at random and have to be slowly pieced back together by whoever is unfortunate enough to be on the receiving end. I mean we were all fluent in Gimponese, basically a few verbs, pronouns and shit loads of fuckology and its variations, fucked, fucker, fuckshitbastard being the main drift. But for people who had never met him before, well, I guess it could be a little disorientating, if not truly terrifying at the same time.

I guess it must be an army thing. All that Sergeant-Major shouting stuff. I mean the Gimp has never really had a normal life. He left school, joined the Army and was sent off to the Falklands to fight other little kids over something – I don't think anyone still really knows what.

He came back to Blighty and I spotted the feral intelligence and deep malicious humour that is my bond with the irritating fucking bastard – and the rest is history.

We've travelled the world annoying the shit out of each other ever since.

To be quite honest I hate leaving England without him. Why? I have no fucking idea. I must love him or something. God. How horrible. Me and the Gimp, till death do us part.

Agghh, pass the suicide!

It was the deadleg shit that brought it all to a horrible, horrible head. Well, horrible for the Gimp. The rest of us thought he got exactly what he deserved.

For fuck's sake, we were the band! He was fucking crew! The bastard didn't seem to understand that though. WE were artistes, HE was a bum with a spanner. The audacity of the man darlings, unbelievable.

"For God's sake Bunty darling, we're simply going to have to do something about little Grizelda, she's getting terribly forward," I said to Cobalt during another pointless rehearsal session, rehearsing our mistakes diligently.

"Shirley, tell me about it petal," said Cobalt.

"Well I'm the singer, I can't possibly lower myself and deal with the hired help, it's going to be have to be down to you Bunts," I said, decking my Pimms cup.

"Any suggestions? Personally I think all this deadlegging business is really *très, très* – God look at my bruises," said the svelte guitarist rolling down his

MARK MANNING

snug leathers.

"I know Bunty darling, I know, cop these," I said, showing him my bruised bottom cheeks.

"Oh my God, that's terrible, when did he get you then?" said my concerned sleazegrinder master.

"In the bloody shower, I had soap in my eyes, the bastard dived in and started punching my arse and legs like a madman. It simply has to stop. What if all our fans find out that were being bullied by a fucking road gremlin? We'll be the laughing stock of rock Bunts, the laughing stock. Who does he bloody think he is anyway? God I'm so cross! Have you seen Cindy's legs!?" (Cindy was Slam's tour name, the drummer simply adored the divine Miss Crawford.)

All of this strange banter was about Gimpo's great joy in giving us dead legs. A brutal punch to the thighs that was excruciatingly painful and took the breath from your lungs. He was skilful at his attacks, usually coming completely out of the blue. Skilful too at avoiding retaliation, twisting out of the way like an oiled newt as you attempted a counter-punch.

Of course the solution to our troublesome problem was simple, brutal and with Nagasaki efficiency, straight to the point. We broke his fucking leg.

We planned it carefully though, like petty little generals in a snidey little war.

I was to distract him with some electrical nonsense while Cobalt charged from the other side of the room and hurled himself knee-first into Grizelda's thigh. With hindsight I think Bunty might have overdone it a little, leaping in like a fucking samurai, knocking the poor bastard to the ground like he'd been hit by an eight-wheeler. The look on the bastard's face though as he collapsed in sheer agony, pure poetry.

The felled Gimp pulled himself by his hands behind an amp, breathless and as white as a fish's belly, gulping for air. He passed out as we all laughed like madmen. His thigh shattered just above the knee.

On crutches for six months, hee hee hee.

Now that's what you call a deadleg.

Nice one Bunty.

ROCKING KILLS

Seeing as how this is going to be the last chapter in my gruesome little confessional, I thought I might as well give some kind of health warning to any potential glamrock warriors out there.

I mean believe it or not, some fucking doughballs actually see me as some kind of a role model.

Imagine having that on your conscience.

I mean I'm probably almost definitely, certainly, maybe completely possibly going to go to Hell when I die.

But you never know, maybe if I try to warn you easily-influenced little rock kids who lurk amongst the foetid newsprint of rubbish magazines about how not to follow in my terrible footsteps, how not to take loads of drugs, shag loads of women and get drunk all the time, I might just make it through the pearly gates, you never know man.

I mean, don't tell any vicars or anything but I sometimes get the impression that God is a bit of a fucking idiot really, I mean look who he's got on his fucking team. All those creepy vicars and dopey black people who thank him at awards ceremonies and stuff.

I mean I reckon if I'm sly enough, I just might be able to bribe my way upstairs. I mean Sting and all those other fuckers seem to have managed it, fucking Bob Geldof, that bogus, dumb arsehole he's even tabloidly been made into some kind of unofficial fucking Saint-type geezer thing.

I mean it seems fucking easy, a few pious promises about never having any fun any more, doing charity things and telling everyone else not to have any fun as well. Maybe I could free Nelson Mandela again, when he gets sent back to jail for blowing up some more innocent people or something.

I mean Lenny Henry, Ben Elton and all those other caring red nose people who humiliate themselves for charity and not to further their flagging, unfunny, bad comedy careers at all. I bet all those fuckers get into Heaven dead easy.

Actually, if Heaven's full of those cocksuckers maybe Bon Scott was right when he was singing about Hell.

Maybe Hell isn't such a bad place to be.

I mean if Heaven is full of Lenny Henrys, Bob Geldofs, Michael Jacksons and all those other kind, considerate, charity marathon insincere wankers, maybe I'd be better off in fucking Hell with Ollie Reed, John Bonham and those other geniuses of the drink.

No, no what am I talking about, there's all that fire and torturing and being bummed by the Devil and stuff.

So here we go, Z's public rocking health warning so that he might not go to Hell when he dies for all his horrible crimes.

And it's addressed to you, little Johnny Rockhead sat in your parental home bedroom with your stash of *Fiestas* and *Razzles* under your bed.

With your cheap little electric guitar with only five strings. With your huge pile of yellowing *NMEs*, *Melody Makers*, *Kerrangs* or whatever other dopey little rock rags kids read these days.

With your socially dysfunctional personality, your spectacles, black T-shirt, spunk stains, acne and greasy hair.

With your chronic masturbation habit and your painful, yearning, burning desire to pork, bone, shag, fuck, bugger and get sucked off by as many fucking birds on this shitty, cruel sexually unfair planet as possible.

With your anger and your loathing, with your fiery unfocused rage.

With your desperate need to get your revenge on every dirty, fucking, bitch, slag, whore that you have ever secretly fallen in love with and never dared ask out in case the bitch slag whore laughed at you and told you to fuck off.

With your radioactive desire to show every one of those loud-mouthed bullying bastards with their stupid gelled hair and shitty sports, dumb Nike, Adidas, mobile phone fashion clothes who seem to get all the best birds and will all end up as fucking whatever their shitty fucking job says they are, that you, Johnny Rockhead, stand way, way above them all.

That you are the king of sexology and shagging, that your dick is a monster, that you can fuck all night and come like an elephant. That you shag SUPERMODELS, TV PRESENTERS AND ACTRESSES!!! Not the dumpy little Tescos till bitches that they pour their spunk into every Friday night after drinking so much that they can't even jizz as you, for the time being anyway, sit wanking lonely in your lonely room where your lonely fucking guitar sits gently fucking wanking too.

But even if I was serious and did try to warn that little social misfit above about the dangers of the rock and roll lifestyle, I reckon my little warning would have about as much of an effect as that pathetic shit they put on the front of fag packets.

Smoking kills, yeah, big deal, fuck off kind of vibe and anyway, everyone knows it's fucking living that kills you, you government doctor arsehole.

I may be many things dear reader, shitheel, arsehole alkie, drug addict, loser, but I'm no fucking hypocrite.

Much.

Unless it kind of benefits me in some sleazy sort of way.

Rocking kills kids.

Yeah? Yeah. I mean it *is* true. Drugs, drink, venal women, all of that shit can and does kill an incredible amount of my rocking *compadres*, far more than anyone realises. For every Kurt Cobain, Jim Morrison and Jimi Hendrix there's a thousand more Arse Ciders and Billy Fuckups from a million bands that no-one ever hears of who, loaded on one substance or another, puke off their mortal coils.

But what a fucking way to go man.

Death by too much fun.

You know what I'm saying.

When you decide to rock, candle at both ends and all that shit, you experience more in one, two, five or however many years you manage to last than almost every safe, pension plan, fridge freezer, Sky TV, two point four kid, one holiday a year motherfucking, newspaper-reading arsewipe does in a whole colonic cancer of a law abiding life, boring, fucking time.

Call me irresponsible if you want, and no doubt a lot of you bloodless, anaemic, jealous arseholes out there will.

But all I can say to you humourless, hypocritical, stupid people who write newspapers and are on television lying and being wankers and stuff is that truly, deeply and almost sincerely,

Mon frère,

Mon lecteur,

I DONT GIVE A FRENCH FLYING FUCK AT A ROLLING FUCKING CROISSANT.

ROCK ON...

–Zodiac Mindwarp, London 2001

POSTSCRIPT:
BAND CHRONOLOGY

Anyone who's eventually managed to wade through these sordid vignettes of lives dumbly lived will appreciate just how hard this part of the whole, alcohol-blackout thing is. I mean, sure I can remember the names of the band members and maybe nearly all the records in just about the right order, but as for tour dates – Jesus Christ, no chance. As you can probably gather from the tales herein, we got royally fucked up in just about all the major – and plenty of the minor – countries and cities in the world, making things such as sequential memory pretty difficult. I'm pretty sure we toured America from New York to LA via every little Shitsburg USA-type hick town at least a couple of times between 1987 and 1988. We trawled every god-forsaken hole in England, Scotland and Wales continuously for a whole decade in ever-decreasing circles, as we did in Northern Europe – especially dear old Deutschland. Those nice German people really seemed to dig the old blitzkrieging sex führer Z and his gang of stormtroopers for some reason – I wonder why.

However, if any of you anal-obsessive whackos out there really think these things are important, there's shitloads of websites compiled by fellow wankologists which can probably help you out. Anyhow, this is about as much as the Stargazer and me can remember – but be warned, we could be wrong.

BAND LINE-UPS

1986/87: Zodiac, Cobalt, Slam Thunderhide, Kid Chaos, + Evil Bastard. Kid left to join The Cult after they bribed him with tours of America, drugs and sex. Can't say I blame him in retrospect seeing we were still on the cider, toilets and speed circuit at the time. Evil ended up in Broadmoor.

1987/88: Zodiac, Cobalt, Slam, Flash Bastard, Trash D. Garbage. Flash and Trash left when the money ran out and went off to compose advertisement music for women's fanny products.

1988: Zodiac, Cobalt, Slam and a cat called Raven from Killing Joke, who left for Brazil after doing something highly illegal.

1988/90: Zodiac, Cobalt, Slam, Suzy X. Slam left after receiving a bottle

across the back of the head from a drunken Stargazer; he now lives in Thailand with a ladyboy.

1990-92: Zodiac, Cobalt, Suzy X, Robbie Vomm. Suzy the logger left to smoke pot all day and compose dance music on a recorder.

1992-96: Zodiac, Cobalt, Robbie, Tex Diablo. Tex left to open a gentlemen's outfitters in Los Angeles.

In 2000 the band was sporadically active again, Zodiac, Cobalt and Robbie joined for some performances by Alex James who then went back to boy band Blur. In 2001 a reunion with Tex was planned, to launch this book at the Viper Room in Los Angeles.

ALBUMS
High Priest Of Love (1986)
Tattooed Beat Messiah (1988)
Hoodlum Thunder (1991)
My Life Story (1993)
One More Knife (1994)

Meanwhile old Z has managed to scrawl a few more books' worth of obscene illiterate filth, in between sitting around watching porno and drinking in his Clerkenwell hovel:

Bible Of Dreams; 1994.
Bad Wisdom; 1996, written with Bill Drummond (Penguin Books).
Crucify Me Again; 1999 (Codex).
Get Your Cock Out!; 2000 (Attack! Books).
Wild Highway; forthcoming, written with Bill Drummond.
Ripper 10, Women 0; forthcoming from Creation Books.

www.creationbooks.com